Understanding Temperament

STRATEGIES FOR CREATING FAMILY HARMONY

Understanding Temperament

STRATEGIES FOR CREATING FAMILY HARMONY

by Lyndall Shick, M.A.

PARENTING PRESS, INC.
Seattle, Washington

Printed in the United States of America

Edited by Carolyn J. Threadgill
Designed by Magrit Baurecht Design
Cover illustration by Jim Hays

ISBN 1-884734-32-4 paperback
ISBN 1-884734-33-2 library binding

Library of Congress Cataloging-in-Publication Data

Shick, Lyndall, 1949–
    Understanding temperament : strategies for creating family
    harmony / by Lyndall Shick. -- 1st ed.
        p.   cm.
    Includes bibliographical references and index.
    ISBN 1-884734-33-2 (lib. bdg.). -- ISBN 1-884734-32-4 (pbk.)
    1. Temperament in children. 2. Individual differences in children.
3. Child rearing. I. Title.
    BF723.T53S55 1998
    649' . 1--dc21   97-36938
                                                            CIP

Parenting Press, Inc.
P.O. Box 75267
Seattle, Washington 98125

Contents

Acknowledgments

redit for the material in this book is due to the people who have pioneered temperament research and who have helped us develop the Temperament Program at the Center for Human Development in LaGrande, Oregon: Dr. Stanley Turecki; Dr. Stella Chess; Dr. Alexander Thomas; Mary Sheedy Kurcinka; the nurses at Arizona State University's temperament project; the staff at Kaiser Permanente Hospital, Oakland, California; and The Preventive Ounce in Berkeley, California. I am also grateful to Bill Smith, Kathy Goodman, Barbara Zukin, Barbara Tyler, and all the people associated with the Center for Parenting Excellence here in LaGrande where I have been a children's mental health therapist. We all collaborated to bring parents this book on temperament and parenting.

One

How This Book Can Help You and Your Family

This book helps you understand your child's temperament. It shows you how to identify and teach the particular skills *your* child needs to meet the demands of the world. The book does not focus on any one type of child, nor does it discuss theory very much. Mostly, it suggests things you can do to parent more effectively, using temperament as a guide. All the strategies honor *both* your temperament and your child's.

The Temperament Program in LaGrande, Oregon started in 1988. It has developed an approach to parenting that can help all parents, regardless of the problems they have rearing their children. This book condenses for you what we have learned from working with hundreds of parents.

Our philosophy is simple:
- Parents know their child better than anyone else does,
- Many factors form personalities,
- "Discipline" is really teaching and learning,
- A useful approach can be found for every child,
- You will not be an instant expert just because you have become a parent.

Parents who adopt a temperament approach to parenting reduce conflicts between themselves and their children. They also create better understanding and stronger ties among family members. Finally, they enjoy their children more!

Regardless of who you are, you have temperament issues to consider: your child's, your own, your spouse or partner's, and perhaps other children's. You can begin to appreciate how complex temperament issues are in families, with a lot of different temperaments coexisting. The ease with which all family members interact demonstrates the "goodness of fit" among parents and children.

Temperament is neither good nor bad. As a set of inborn traits, it is much like having brown eyes or blue ones. It is just the way we are. Although we can learn to modify our trait-based impulses as we age, our basic temperamental make-up remains the same throughout our lives. Our temperament has a great deal to do with how we behave and with how others perceive us. Temperament traits make some situations easy for us, and other situations difficult. It can be a struggle to learn the behaviors that are contrary to our temperaments. It is good to give your child an early start because these skills will smooth his or her way through life.

Some parents have a challenging child. This is a child who has a constellation of traits that make life difficult for him and those who live with him and try to shape his behavior. Parenting books have focused on this type of child because he or she is disruptive, tries everyone's patience, and virtually demands attention. Parents are, understandably, at their wits' end, desperate for help.

The focus of *Understanding Temperament* is not solely the challenging child, although the ideas here are useful for understanding and working with him or her. Rather, I want to talk about the many ways that children are different and how those differences affect life in a family. Even though challenging children are the squeaky wheels that get the grease, there are many "easy" children who have needs every bit as urgent as those of the challenging child. Unfortunately, the needs of easy children are often invisible. These children may not make their needs, or even themselves, known in their families. Parents may wrongly assume that the child is doing well because he or she is quiet, seems well adjusted, and poses no behavior problems at home, at school, or in the community. In fact, easy children pose unique challenges to parents. As you will see, these children need to learn some valuable skills, too.

With the help of this book, you will learn how to incorporate temperament knowledge into your parenting style and goals. You will be able to change attitudes and behaviors with new approaches. You will also learn how to teach your children useful, lifelong skills.

Two

Parenting with Temperament in Mind

Temperament is a set of ten traits that explains the "how" of behavior. It determines the way a person reacts in a given situation. Your child's temperament, to a large degree, determines the kind of interactions you have many times a day in your family. Temperament also determines the kinds of parenting your child will need to grow and develop in the best, most individual way for him or her. An understanding of temperament helps you tailor your parenting to the individual needs of your unique child.

Effective Parents

Finding ways to channel your child's inner strengths to promote healthy development is an enormous challenge. All children are full of untapped potential waiting to be realized. The goal is to find ways to parent that fit your own style and also work with your child's very individual temperament.

Effective parents are those who:
- Are flexible,
- Understand what makes their child "tick,"
- Learn from mistakes while they avoid repeating them,
- Feel good about themselves,
- Know there are no pat answers to most dilemmas of child rearing,
- Do not expect perfection from themselves or their child,
- Create new strategies as the child grows up,
- Do not rely on the same old techniques year in and year out,
- Give up guilt and blame—of their child, of each other, and of themselves,
- Have a sense of humor,
- Remember that they too were once young, and
- Respect themselves and their child.

You may feel that making changes to your parenting style based on your child's temperament is a lot of trouble, or seems like "spoiling" your child. Yes, changes take effort and thought. However, if you think of these changes simply as ways to avoid unnecessary conflicts, they make more sense. They are worth the effort if they make your life and your child's easier. An added bonus is that as you honor your child's individuality, you model and teach that you value differences in people; you teach respect for others by respecting your child.

Development Versus Temperament

Be careful not to confuse a developmental phase with a temperament trait. Development moves through stages and is dictated by natural growth mechanisms: metabolism, hormones, stimulation, expectations, and experience. Development will override temperament. For instance, a typical nine-month-old baby is usually afraid of strangers. The child is not being shy or cautious in approaching other people. She is going through a normal developmental phase called "stranger anxiety." Temperamentally, she may actually be very outgoing, both before she hit this phase and after she passes through it.

Temperament colors *how* your baby does everything. For instance, all babies learn to make sounds. How they do so will depend on their intensity, sensory awareness, and persistence. Similarly, all babies learn to walk. How they go about it will depend on their activity level and persistence. Temperament theory compliments developmental theory and fleshes out our understanding of each child's individuality. Developmental knowledge helps you have realistic expectations for your child.

Goodness of Fit

Children grow when the demands and expectations of their parents, other important people in their lives, and life circumstances are compatible with their temperaments, abilities, and other characteristics. While parents cannot change their child's temperament, they can, to some extent, control the environment in which he lives and the experiences he has. They can teach the skills that will help him meet the demands of his environment. They can accept the child's individual style of behavior, provide a loving environment that encourages learning, and offer specific ways to develop and practice needed skills. Parents can also improve the fit between child and teacher, child and care providers, and child and family members. Often, parents can improve the fit between their child and his or her physical environment, as well.

Time Is on Your Side

If you feel overwhelmed by these suggestions, remember that your child will live with you for many years and you have a long time in which to work. Other people can help, too. Parenting is a big job, and you do not need to do it all at once or all alone. Children are "works in progress."

Tips to Remember

1. Your job is easier when you tailor your parenting to your child's temperament.
2. Development is about growth; temperament is about style.
3. Children grow best when there is a good fit between their temperament and the demands of their environment.

Three

The Ten
Temperament Traits

Ten traits make up a temperament profile. If you have read much
about temperament, you may have seen slight variations in the
ten traits, and that is all right. This trait list is one of several,
which all provide a good basis for assessing a person's temperament.
Briefly, the traits are:

- Activity
- Adaptability
- Approach
- Distractibility
- Emotional sensitivity
- Intensity
- Mood

- Persistence
- Regularity
- Sensory awareness

Here are the ten traits and some stories that illustrate them.

Activity

This trait relates to how much physical energy the child expends. Left to her own devices, would your child be in motion or still? Would she rather run or sit? Video games and television aside, ask yourself what your child would prefer to be doing, given a choice between activity and repose.

One frazzled couple came in to our parenting center with a two-and-a-half-year-old boy, asking for help. In a matter of minutes while parents and counselor talked, the child rearranged the entire office to create a fort for himself out of the furniture. Everyone agreed this couple needed help!

While on a home visit, I watched a tiny girl bounce and jiggle her way to the kitchen counter, climb the refrigerator, open the freezer compartment and then a drawer, get out a spoon and a bowl, and dish up a big serving of ice cream, all in the time it took me to sit down and start talking with her parents.

Another high activity, positive mood, high approach two-year-old crept from bed while his parents slept and pushed a chair up to the kitchen counter. He then climbed up onto the counter top and stepped into the sink. His foot fit neatly into the drain opening and rested on the garbage disposal blades. He was reaching for the disposal switch when his dad appeared in the doorway and distracted him—preventing him from grinding his foot off in the disposal. Another unforgettable moment in family history!

Low activity kids pose different challenges. Consider the third grader who simply hates anything to do with physical activity. The child who comes to mind was born into a family of very active people. They ski, ride horses, teach jazzercise classes, swim laps, hike, camp, hunt, fish, and go out for every sport imaginable. This child does not want to do any of those things. He wants to sit on the couch and read. He also likes the family computer. His sedentary habits cause problems for his parents, who must decide whether to force him to come along, leave another family member home to watch him, or hire a sitter. Because he hates activity, he has not practiced the physical skills that the rest of the kids mastered early on. Consequently, he is uncoordinated, not very physically fit, and ignorant about how to play games or do activities. These handicaps cause him to resist participating more adamantly now than he did as a younger child. His parents say the whole thing has snowballed into a big source of conflict.

Adaptability

This trait relates to how easily the child adjusts to transitions or changes. Does he go with the flow or kick and scream when changes are imposed on him? Ask, how quickly or slowly does my child adjust to changes when they are not his idea?

One second grader with very low adaptability hated every change suggested by anyone but herself. Her mother says, "Jessie could be counted on to think any new idea was a bad one. We could be planning a weekend full of activities, and she would play resident curmudgeon, scowling and objecting to every suggestion. Her low adaptability cuts her off from new experiences she needs to share with us in order to be a part of our lives."

Approach

This trait refers to how the child reacts to new things, places, and people. Does she readily accept and even seek out newness, or resist and hold back? Ask yourself, what is my child's usual first reaction to new people, situations, and places?

The mother of a very slow-to-approach child walked through a mall with her child, where she ran into an old friend from school whom she had not seen for many years. She wanted her daughter to say hello to her friend, but the little girl was shy and would not. In her enthusiasm, the friend bent down and put her face right up next to the child's. In response, the child, who was not ready to make contact with this stranger and felt threatened, shouted, "Get away from me, you witch!" Her mother was horrified.

Children with quick-to-approach tendencies can create especially memorable moments, too. A little boy wandered into a horse corral and sat down in the dirt. When his frantic parents found him, he was sitting happily in the midst of a dozen whirling horses, hooves and dust flying, laughing and waving his arms in glee. The horses had not stepped on him or even bumped him, but his folks will never forget their fear for their child.

Distractibility

This trait has to do with how easily your child shifts attention when interruptions occur. Highly distractible children forget what they were doing before they finish. They may also be able to do several things at once. Ask, does he get sidetracked by sounds and not listen to what you said? Can you easily distract him from upset feelings or undesirable activity by redirecting his attention?

Low distractibility can cause people to wonder if a child notices what goes on around him. Norman, a young student, once sat at his desk long after the rest of the children had gone out to recess. Thinking something was wrong, the teacher approached him, put her hand on his arm, and asked what was the matter. Startled, Norman replied that he was still thinking about something inside his head, and had not noticed the others were gone. He was so focused, in fact, that he had not heard the bell, the kids leaving, or the sounds on the busy playground just outside the window. This tremendous concentration was both a liability and a talent. This same child grew up and went away to college. He and another boy from his hometown moved into co-op housing. Sam, Norman's friend, hated it. He was going crazy. He couldn't think, let alone study. There was partying, kids rough-housing, loud music, girls in and out, and all of the things that go on in a place full of eighteen-year-olds on their own for the first time. Sam barely lasted the first term. Concerned, Norman's parents asked if he, too, wanted to find different housing for winter term, to which Norman replied, "Mom, it's okay for me. I just go into my head and shut it all out. I can study fine."

Emotional Sensitivity

How readily does your child feel his own and others' emotions? Emotional sensitivity is an inside reaction, unlike intensity, which is the outside manner of expressing emotions. Ask, does my child often become upset "over nothing" or does he rarely become upset even when circumstances suggest that he could? Does the child feel sympathy and empathy with others who are experiencing strong emotions?

Highly emotionally sensitive children like Kelly, a young boy who had difficulty watching Disney movies, can become overwhelmed by powerful scenes in films or news reports. These people often find ways to reduce their discomfort. Some will close their eyes or cover their ears during disturbing scenes. Others will take a mental fantasy trip to avoid parts they find unbearable. Still others leave the room. Kelly, with his incredible sensitivity, majored in drama as a young adult, and became a teacher and an actor.

Children with lower emotional sensitivity behave differently than their more sensitive peers. Teenager Brenda was able to make all the arrangements for a memorial service for another teen killed in a car accident. Grief did not make her unable to think and act, even though she knew the victim well. Although saddened, she was able to talk with the parents without undue distress. She could plan all the details of a service without falling apart as several of her friends were doing.

Intensity

This trait refers to how strongly the child reacts to things, both positive and negative. Intense children are often dramatic. They put a great deal of energy into expressing their feelings. They seem passionate, animated, highly emotional, and expressive. Ask yourself, can I easily tell what my child is feeling, or is it difficult to know what is happening inside?

One highly intense little fellow, upset by the slow arrival of his Thanksgiving dinner, furrowed his brow, turned red in the face, opened his mouth as wide as it would go, and let out a terrific yowl. There was no doubt about his frustration! His response was pure intensity.

Low intensity is just the opposite. You may not be able to tell how your child feels. A highly intense father gleefully planned and saved and eventually purchased a perfectly beautiful china doll. He believed his daughter wanted this doll more than anything else. He took great satisfaction in imagining her joy in receiving his gift. When Christmas morning finally arrived, the child carefully opened the present, politely said thank you, and put the doll up. Her father was crestfallen, interpreting her minimal response as lack of interest or gratitude. In fact, the doll deeply impressed her, but her low intensity meant that she did not demonstrate her feelings in a way that her high intensity father could recognize.

Mood

This trait refers to whether the child views the world with optimism (positively) or with pessimism (negatively). Ask yourself, is my child's overall attitude sunny or gloomy? Does she view the world through rose-colored glasses? Does she see the proverbial glass half empty or half full? Does she usually see the good in a situation first, or the bad?

Two middle school-aged sisters, flying home after spending the summer with their father, arrived at the baggage claim area to find that the airline had lost their luggage. One sister, unfazed, announced to her mother that maybe someone who needed the stuff more than she did would get it, and anyway, she would have fun shopping to replace the essentials. Her sister, on the other hand, immediately became angry and complained for days about her lost belongings and the incompetence and untrustworthiness of airline employees. The sisters' different perceptions of this event were dictated by the trait of mood.

Persistence

This trait refers to how long a child will keep at a task after it becomes difficult or boring. Highly persistent children will lock in on an activity; those with low persistence will give up or call for help when they become frustrated. Ask, does my child stick with things even after they're no fun anymore?

Highly persistent children are known for being champion naggers. Count the number of times your child will come back and ask over and over again for the same thing. Some children can do it literally dozens of times.

Low persistence children give up their efforts very quickly. One mom vented her frustration over a little guy who refused to make more than one attempt at tying his shoes. If he did not get them tied on the first try, it was all over. He would yell for help. At this rate, it took him a long time to master the skill he needed.

Regularity

This trait refers to how predictable a child's biological functions are within a twenty-four-hour period. This includes hunger, sleep, and elimination cycles. Ask, does my child normally tend to eat, sleep, awaken, or have a bowel movement at predictable times each day?

Irregularity creates demands on families for flexibility in eating and sleeping schedules. I know of a large family that felt this most on vacations. The other family members were regular and could easily agree on when to stop to eat. Rachel, however, was highly irregular. She wasn't hungry at the times everyone else was. She would refuse food at the restaurant, only to wail that she was starving an hour and a half later. To avoid having to stop again, her mom began wrapping up some food and keeping it handy. At night on camping trips everyone would be ready to crawl into their sleeping bags, but not Rachel. She would be wide awake. The solution was to give her a flashlight, coloring books, and crayons, and let her entertain herself until she was sleepy.

Sensory Awareness

This trait, which relates to how acute each of our senses is, has a rating scale for each of the five senses. Some children are over stimulated by sensory input. They have high sensory awareness. Others hardly notice sensory stimuli. They have low sensory awareness. Ask yourself, how aware is my child of noises, temperature changes, lights, colors, odors, flavors, or textures? How does he respond to pain and to light touch? Consider each sense separately, as it is possible to be highly sensitive in one sense and not at all sensitive in another.

A mom introduced her baby to solid foods. She said, "I put a whole pea in my daughter's mouth, and she rolled it around on her tongue and felt it and then she just laughed and laughed and laughed. She had tears running down her cheeks she laughed so hard at this pea and the shape and texture of it. I thought what a funny thing, to be so delighted by a pea! Now I can tell you it was her sensory awareness that made her react that way."

Low sensory awareness is illustrated by the story of the mother who took her child to the pediatrician for a sore throat. As he examined the throat, the doctor scolded the mother, saying he could not believe she had waited so long to bring the child in. He just could not imagine letting something go this far without attending to it. He insisted the throat was extremely painful to the child, and implied that failing to seek treatment sooner bordered on medical neglect. What he failed to understand was that this child never mentioned discomfort at all. Her mother took her in after she noticed foul breath and enlarged tonsils. Because of the child's low sensory awareness for pain, she simply didn't notice or tell anyone until the infection was quite advanced. Oddly, this is the same child who was exquisitely sensitive to texture and shape and taste—the baby who was so delighted by the feel of her first whole pea.

The mother of a kindergarten-aged son related how his high sensory awareness to light touch affected him. The child had two identical pairs of pants he would wear. They were soft, worn corduroy with all the tags cut out. One morning, both of his acceptable pants were in the wash. His mom did her best to get him into another pair of pants, but was unsuccessful. He could not tolerate the feel of different pants, and ended up staying home that day.

Other children with high sensory awareness use a pleasing fabric to comfort themselves. We all know children who enjoy stroking satin blanket binding or fuzzy materials in times of distress. One mother recounted having to leave her baby in the hospital overnight. He screamed and reached for her, and it was all she could do to separate from him. The nurse was firm: Mom had to go. In desperation, she pulled the silk scarf from around her neck and gave it to the shrieking baby. Some combination of smell and warmth and texture instantly quieted him. He thrust his thumb in his mouth, pressed the scarf to his face, and became drowsy. She was then able to leave the hospital. This boy named the scarf his "fluffy" and carried it for several years. Each time one wore out, his mother replaced it from her wardrobe. He went through many "fluffies" before he was ready to let them go.

These are the ten temperament traits we will talk about in this book. They profoundly affect family life. There are many strategies parents can use to help life run more smoothly and enable their children to grow to their potential.

Tips to Remember

1. The ten temperament traits combine in different ways to make each member of your family unique.
2. A child who is very high *or* very low in a particular trait may be challenging.
3. Children may show high sensory awareness for one sense but not others.

Four

Why Parents and Children Clash

Many families find themselves caught up in a vicious cycle of negative interactions with their children. The cycle fuels itself. The child disobeys, the parent punishes, the child reacts to the punishment, the parent reacts to the child's reaction, and on and on. Everyone involved becomes angry and frustrated. An otherwise pleasant day is ruined for the whole family. Some families have these days now and then and see them as mere skirmishes. Others have one problem after another and feel that they live in a war zone.

The Clash

Sometimes a clash between the child's temperament and your parenting style sets the cycle in motion. Imagine for a moment a child who is by nature slow to adapt, negative in mood, and highly intense. This child did not, we must remind ourselves, select these traits for herself any more than she chose to have brown eyes and blond hair. Nevertheless, they are hers for a lifetime. Now imagine a parent who is quick to adapt, average in mood, and who has a low intensity level. Are you beginning to see the many opportunities for trouble?

Picture this scene: A child is absorbed in a favorite television show. Her mother must suddenly run an unexpected errand. She says to the child, "Get your coat, honey, we have to get downtown quickly before the post office closes!" A different child might see this as an adventure. Not this one. She sees it as an intolerable intrusion. She protests. Her mom has no one who can watch her daughter and must take her along. The child begins to cry, then to throw a tantrum. Mom cannot understand at all how the child is perceiving the interruption. Mom feels put upon and annoyed. They tussle over putting on the coat. Mom clicks off the television, and the child wails louder yet. In exasperation, Mom grabs the child by the arm and hauls her to the car, where she buckles her into her car seat and demands, "Stop this fuss, right now!"

In temperament terms, what is going on here? This little girl cannot help her initial reaction to a sudden demand to change activities. It is a part of her basic, slow-to-adapt nature. She is as sure to react badly to imposed changes as she would be to sneeze at cat dander if she were allergic to it. Her negative mood causes her to see things as worse than they are. Her high intensity causes her to put a lot of energy into expressing her emotions. A temper tantrum is the natural result of her temperament and a situation which challenges several strong traits.

She is not being deliberately obstinate. She does not want to make a problem for her mother. Nevertheless, the demand to stop what she is doing, put on her coat, and get in the car goes against her idea of what should be happening at that moment. You may have difficulty understanding her reactions unless you share her traits. A slow-to-adapt mom probably would refuse to run an unexpected, last minute errand, and the conflict with the child would never occur. This mom, however, does not resist the demand for a sudden transition because it seems okay to her.

Like the mother's in the story, your requests to your child seem reasonable to you. However, simple things can get big reactions if they are contrary to temperament. Asking one child to stay in his chair, shake hands with Mr. Miller, or eat a strange new food can result in tears and tantrums. To another child, these requests would pose no problem. To a child with a high activity level, staying seated is hard. To one with low approach, shaking hands is frightening. To one with low adaptability, a new food on the plate can create a crisis. When strong natural preferences are involved, each request poses a serious difficulty.

The Vicious Cycle

Out of desperation, parents may punish a child for behaving like the slow-to-adapt girl in the story. Such punishment does not work, because trait-based responses are not successfully changed this way. Without an understanding of temperament, it is easy for parents to attribute misbehavior to all sorts of naughty motivations on the child's part. When this happens, parents either increase the amount and kind of punishment, or give up and label the child a "brat" or worse. Either way, the child does not comply. The parent becomes increasingly frustrated and angry.

Frustration fuels the vicious cycle. It is normal for both you and your child to feel frustrated. You are trying very hard to help your child behave. It seems that nothing works. You may be following expert advice, or doing things that worked with your other children—and this child is still resistant and uncooperative. You may be at the end of your rope.

Each time the vicious cycle is set in motion, it becomes more habitual. The more it happens, the more likely it is to happen again. You end up constantly battling with your child. This can lead to a sense of despair.

Now is the time to remember that there is nothing wrong with you, and there is nothing wrong with your child. The way you are interacting with your child is simply not working. When we feel frustrated and stressed, we act differently than we would normally. We may yell at the child, who yells back at us. We may say things we do not really mean, and the child may do the same. Who has not reflected painfully on the long-lasting effects of angry, hurtful words, uttered in a few regrettable seconds, that can never be taken back?

As stress increases, so do other problems. As other problems come up, stress increases. And so it goes. When the vicious cycle really gets going, it can affect all areas of your life at once.

The Solution

Understanding your child's temperament is the foundation for stopping this cycle and learning new parenting skills that work. The strategies in this book show you how to stop. When you do, you will notice a change in how your whole family interacts and in how you feel. Some parents notice their child is happier, more coopera-tive, and more fun to be around. The emotional tone in your home will become more positive. Everyone in the family gets along bet-ter. You will have more time and energy to deal with your child in constructive ways. You will be able to teach values, honest com-munication, and social skills. You may also work on important things with your child like feeling good about himself, succeeding in school, and practicing healthy ways to relate to people.

Once the war is over, you can focus on these and other impor-tant goals. As you do this, you will be working toward "goodness of fit."

Goodness of Fit

Goodness of fit is the compatibility between your child and the environment. You are a big part of that environment. With the "easy" child, there is a lucky match. Your style, your spouse's style, and the expectations of life in your home all harmonize with the child's temperament.

Some families have several "easy" children and one difficult or challenging child who seems to demand more than his or her share of parental time and attention. If you are one of these families, you have noticed that "treating them all the same" is not effective. What works for one child will not work for the other. Some children seem to be in almost nonstop conflict with their parents, while others nearly never are. With your challenging child, there is an unfortunate mismatch, and there is discord between you. It is not that you did anything right or wrong with either of your children. They were simply born different. Also, a child may have a good fit in one place or with one set of people, and a poor fit somewhere else. Some temperaments fit better in certain environments than in others.

Temperament-based conflict often creates long-lasting impressions. A friend recalls her own childhood, in which a difference in approach caused problems. Her mother is high approach. She is low approach. She says, "Learning about temperament was freeing for me. I had always thought there was something wrong with me—or at least I got the message from my mother that she thought there was something wrong with me—and now I can see that it was a simple matter of temperament style. Mom was always pushing me out into the world to try new things and meet new people. And I frustrated her by hanging back. She gets her energy from interacting with people in new situations. She travels easily in foreign countries, participates in theater productions, and generally puts herself in the middle of whatever is going on. I, on the other hand, prefer to keep a lower profile, to check things out carefully before getting involved. There was a poor fit between us." Each time this friend's mother told her to step forward, look 'em in the eye, shake hands, and say, "I'm pleased to meet you" she challenged her daughter's temperament. The child's natural first impulse was to hide! Sometimes hurt feelings result from temperament differences.

How to Improve the Fit

Fortunately, you can influence your child's environment to improve the fit by the ways you handle your own responses and the approaches you use as you interact with her. You can also alter schedules and physical surroundings to better fit her temperament. For example, if your child is highly active, you can put breakables up out of reach. If your child's sensory awareness is very keen, you can cut scratchy tags out of her clothing. If your child is highly intense and tends to be loud, you can quiet her by turning down the volume in the home. If your child is highly distractible, you can minimize diversions in her surroundings.

As you progress through this book, you will learn many things you can do to improve the fit between your child and his or her environment.

Tips to Remember

1. Family problems may have their origins in temperament clashes between parent and child, or sibling and sibling.
2. Understanding temperament helps you stop the cycle of frustration, blame, and battle.
3. You *can* improve the goodness of fit for all the members of your family once you apply your understanding of temperament to the problems that arise.

Five

What Is Your Child's Temperament?

The first step in using temperament knowledge to improve the atmosphere in your home is to figure out your child's temperament. Someone who knows the child well is the best person to assess her temperament. Most often, the person who first picks up this book is the primary caretaker and knows the child best. If you live with the child, you are qualified to make a good assessment. You are the expert on her. You have been observing her natural first reactions since she came into your home. Your assessment is the basis for devising parenting strategies that fit her. You are about to discover the origins of your child's behavior! As you define her temperament, you will understand not only the "why" of how she reacts, but also the "how" of managing those reactions effectively.

The following pages contain temperament trait descriptions and rating scales for each trait. Please do this with another adult who also knows your child well. You might use different-colored pens to keep your ratings separate. You may each have different perceptions of the child's temperaments. That is okay. It just means that you perceive the child from your own temperament. This explains why sometimes one parent is driven nearly to distraction by a trait that the other parent scarcely notices. This happens when we share a trait with the child. These differences in perception will provide valuable opportunities for discussion. You will probably come away with a better understanding of yourselves as well as a more complete picture of the child. If you cannot decide how to rate a trait, remember the child at a younger age. Ask yourself, generally how does she act? If you are still stuck, assign a mid-range rating. Extremely high or low manifestations of traits stand out clearly; behaviors falling mid-range are less noticeable.

Activity

A child's overall preference for active or inactive play; a child's overall energy level throughout the day.

Best clue: Leaving television and video games aside, what things would your child do if left to his own devices? Would he be "on the go" or idle?

Low activity
Calm and slow moving   **High activity**
                                            Wild and quick moving

Adaptability

How easily a child adjusts to attempts to influence what she is doing or thinking.

Best clue: Does your child adapt quickly to changes, new places, ideas, expectations? Is it difficult or easy for your child when there is a new routine or schedule?

Fast adapting
Easygoing   **Slow adapting**
                                                                   Strong willed

Approach

A child's initial tendency for responding to a new experience, a new person, or a new environment.

Best clue: What is your child's first and usual reaction to new people, situations, or places?

Quick approach
Outgoing/Eager   **Slow approach**
                                       Slow to warm up/Withdrawing

Distractibility

How easily things going on around him interrupt a child's thought processes or attention.

Best clue: Is your child very aware and easily diverted by noises and people? Does he get sidetracked from what you said when something else catches his attention? Can you distract him from upset feelings by redirecting his attention?

Low distractibility
Not easily diverted   **High distractibility**
                                                       Easily diverted

Emotional Sensitivity

The ease or difficulty with which a child responds emotionally to a situation. This trait has two sub-scales, one for sensitivity to one's own feelings and one for sensitivity to others' feelings.

Best clue: Does your child often become upset "over nothing" or does she rarely become upset even when circumstances suggest that she could? Does the child feel sympathy for or empathy with others?

Self

Insensitive to own feelings
Unaware of emotions

Highly sensitive
Feels own emotions strongly

Others

Insensitive to others' feelings
Emotionally tuned out

Highly sensitive
Emotionally tuned in

Intensity

The amount of energy a child commonly uses to express emotions.

Best clue: How physically dramatic, fierce, or passionate is your child when expressing strong feeling? Is he easy or hard to "read?"

Low intensity
Mild reactions

High intensity
Dramatic reactions

Mood

The amount of pleasant, joyful, and friendly behavior as contrasted with unpleasant, crying, and unfriendly behavior.

Best clue: Does your child tend to view the world as primarily a positive or primarily a negative place? Is she an optimist or a pessimist? Light-hearted or serious?

Positive mood
Happy-go-lucky/Optimistic

Negative mood
Somber/Pessimistic

Persistence

The length of time a child will continue to make an effort, especially when the task gets hard.

Best clue: Does he stick with things even when frustrated? Can he stop an activity when asked to?

High persistence
Gets "locked in"

Low persistence
Stops easily

Regularity

The day-to-day predictability of hunger, sleep, and elimination. Consider each function separately, and rate it on its own scale.

Best clue: Does your child normally tend to go to bed, wake up, or have bowel movements at the same time each day?

Hunger

Wants food at same time

Irregular eater

Sleep

Tired on schedule

No schedule

Elimination

BM's at same time daily

Try and guess

Sensory Awareness

How sensitive a child is in each of her sensory channels: 1) pain, 2) touch, 3) taste, 4) smell, 5) hearing, and 6) sight. You rate each channel on a separate scale.

Best clue: How aware of noises, temperature changes, lights, odors, flavors, and textures is your child? How does she respond to pain? It is possible for a child to be very aware in some channels and unaware in others.

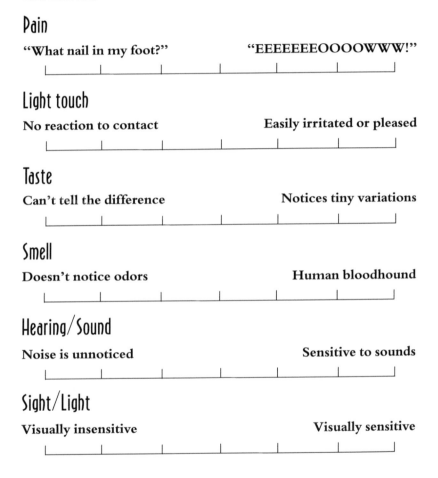

Pain

"What nail in my foot?"   **"EEEEEEEOOOOWWW!"**

Light touch

No reaction to contact   **Easily irritated or pleased**

Taste

Can't tell the difference   **Notices tiny variations**

Smell

Doesn't notice odors   **Human bloodhound**

Hearing/Sound

Noise is unnoticed   **Sensitive to sounds**

Sight/Light

Visually insensitive   **Visually sensitive**

You have finished all ten traits. Now go over your ratings with your spouse or partner and compare how you scored the items. Discuss possible reasons for your differences. Do you spend different amounts of time with the child? Different parts of the day? In different settings? Are your own temperaments quite different from the child's? From each other's? Mark the assessment pages in the book so you can refer back to them easily.

Tips to Remember

1. Knowledge of your child's temperament will explain much of his or her behavior to you.
2. You will gain more insight when you *write down* and *share* your observations of your child's temperament with someone else who knows him or her.
3. *Posting* the short version of the temperament chart in places where you interact most often with your child will help you remember to parent with temperament in mind.

Six

Strengths Based in Temperament

Mysterious behavior becomes understandable when you know your child's temperament. You also have the opportunity to look at aspects of your child's nature that seemed to be weaknesses but, in fact, are strengths. As you focus on strengths, you will gain understanding and compassion, and consequently strengthen your relationship with your child. Whatever the trait, whether you rated it high or low, you will find blessings associated with it. Some traits are more challenging than others, but each one has a positive side.

Activity

Low activity children may excel at quiet indoor tasks. In the future, they will be perfectly happy at desk jobs where they do not have to move around much. They tend to be contemplative and seldom become "stir-crazy."

Their high activity siblings, by contrast, will have energy for strenuous physical tasks and a natural tendency towards physical fitness, participating in sports and doing many different activities.

A highly active child can wear you out, but that same energy will allow the child to accomplish a lot in life. Highly active kids often grow up to be very successful in their careers. They are the kind of adults who work hard and play hard. Their lives are very full.

Adaptability

Slow-to-adapt children are not easily led. As adolescents, they do not yield to peer pressure as readily as their more adaptable siblings. They tend to think for themselves, and to look carefully before they go along with something new or strange.

Adaptable children have an easy time getting along in changing environments. They "go with the flow" and seem to accept whatever life sends them.

Approach

Slow-to-approach children can be frustrating, always hanging back and clinging to your knees. On the other hand, they are unlikely to rush into dangerous situations or take undue risks. They are cautious, tend to think things through, and do not behave rashly in later life. Slow-to-approach children will be cautious around strangers and carefully check out a situation before getting involved in it. They can be, however, just as friendly and outgoing as the quick-to-approach children once they are familiar with new people and surroundings.

Quick-to-approach children will make new friends quickly and join in easily with groups. They will never be left out.

Distractibility

A child who is hard to distract will have an easy time maintaining concentration on complex tasks. She will be able to function in a busy environment, overlooking ringing telephones, barking dogs, and chatting co-workers.

The easily distracted child will not hang on to worry, upset, or anger. She will refocus her emotional attention easily. This means she will not hold on to old issues for long. This child lives in the present moment, involved with whatever is happening right NOW.

Emotional Sensitivity

Emotionally sensitive children will tune in to their own and perhaps to others' feelings as well, making them considerate and empathetic.

Emotionally insensitive children are unencumbered by emotion. They are free to get on with the business at hand. Very little will be a "big deal" to these children. They are untroubled by feelings, and bounce back fast from life's painful experiences.

Intensity

Low intensity children are easy-going and comfortable for others to be around. They do not overreact, make a big fuss, or display feelings overtly. They may be quiet or noisy, but they appear to be on an even keel. They do not inflict their emotional states on others. They keep their own counsel.

High intensity children will be enthusiastic, even passionate about much in their lives. They are naturally dramatic and may excel at acting, public speaking, or comedy. They become wholeheartedly involved in causes in which they believe. It is usually obvious what emotional state they are in.

A comparison of the Japanese people to the Italian people shows that some traits can be representative of whole cultures, not just individuals. A highly intense group of Italians described their discomfort at visiting with a business group comprised of very low intensity Japanese people: "We just couldn't tell what, if anything, was going on. When we told a joke, they didn't laugh. They just smiled politely." The Japanese were equally mystified by the boisterous behavior of the Italians.

Mood

A child with optimistic mood will see good all around her. She will be trusting, cheerful, and seldom depressed.

Pessimistic mood children are careful, analytical, and hard to take in or fool. Such a child may say "no," rather than trust blindly.

Persistence

Highly persistent children can stick with jobs until they finish. They have the staying power to complete complex projects.

Children with low persistence become good at finding efficient ways of doing things so that they can get the job done quickly. They quit when it makes sense to do so, rather than getting locked in on something and continuing past the point of common sense.

Regularity

Children with high regularity may be easy to toilet train. They are inclined to have eating and sleeping habits which promote well-being. They sleep at the same times each 24-hour period, and you can set your clock by their hunger cycles. One lucky mom reported that both her babies slept eight-and-a-half hours a night from the first night home from the hospital! As teens, they continue this pattern. These children will be comfortable with a schedule that remains the same.

Children with low regularity, on the other hand, will adjust to flexible schedules easily, and not be bound by the clock for meals or sleep.

Sensory Awareness

Children with high sensory awareness are able to detect subtle differences. They may have perfect pitch, or be future wine or coffee tasters. They are the natural "quality control experts." They can be exquisitely discerning in one or more sensory channels.

Children with low sensory awareness, on the other hand, will not be particular about things. They do not notice if the food does not taste the same way twice and they are not bothered if things are not "just right." They may be easy to please, uncritical, and accepting.

Take the Long View

It is especially helpful for parents to think of a child's temperament in terms of how it will affect her adult life. Your imagination will help you see most clearly the assets and liabilities of her temperament. As you imagine her in adulthood, think about her traits in terms of what will serve her well and what may require some adapting.

We adults, unlike children, are largely in control of which environments we seek out and which we avoid. We tend to arrange our lives so that the strengths of our temperaments are maximized and the weaknesses are minimized. For example, if you are a calm, very regular person who is not very persistent, you probably would not choose to become an emergency medical technician. Nothing about such an intense, erratic, and difficult job would appeal to you! In fact, you would find much of the job very unpleasant. Instead, you might choose a position with predictable, fixed work hours, in a quiet, calm place with work made up of a series of short tasks. Since our kids cannot yet choose their surroundings or activities, it makes sense that we try to minimize their discomfort whenever we can.

Change Behavior Through Teaching

It takes time to change temperament-based behaviors, a necessity when adaptation is in the child's best interest. Parents must teach skills that are difficult for their child to master because they are not natural to her. Some skills may actually oppose what comes naturally. For example, the skill of taking part in aerobic exercise is hard for a low activity child, and the skill of meeting and greeting new people is painful for a slow-to-approach child to master.

Effective Teaching

Most parents feel that they are responsible for getting their child to cooperate. Some feel criticized by other people for failing to do so. Consequently, when the child misbehaves, they may resort to harsh means of punishment. The thought that parents are responsible *only for making their best effort and may not necessarily succeed,* may reduce guilty feelings. After all, it is the child's task to grow up and learn to behave appropriately. Short of using force or threat of force, it is practically impossible to *make* anyone do anything. It is far better to lead and teach than to force children, who then become resentful, learn coercive methods, and begin forcing those smaller than themselves. As you teach and the child learns, behavior will gradually change.

Good discipline teaches children the rules people live by and helps them practice those rules. Teaching *by example* is a powerful method, because children imitate the behavior they see. Most parents know that kids end up "doing what we do" more often than they "do what we say." The best combination is when what we do and what we say are the same.

When parents create a relationship built on respect, understanding, and shared enjoyment, they have a good chance of being effective teachers. When they create a relationship built on power and control, they have a poorer chance of being effective teachers. In parenting, as in most relationships, the child will usually match your output. So, anger begets anger, hurtfulness begets hurtfulness, kindness begets kindness, trust begets trust. Many children will let you set the tone of interactions and follow suit.

A noted foster mother, a woman in her 80's, has helped raise several hundred children over the past 50 years. She has the ability to calm the most difficult children by her mere presence. Violent, hyperactive, ill-mannered, even delinquent kids are transformed into polite, cooperative, and reasonable people under her influence. How does she accomplish this feat? She is consistently respectful of who the child is, and calm, firm, and loving toward that child. Even the most damaged children respond positively. If this woman's respect can elicit such response from the toughest of kids, just think what possibilities exist for your home and family once you make changes based on *really* knowing your child.

Negative energy will almost certainly elicit the same from your child. Positive energy will elicit positive response. Mood somewhat determines the response your child gives back. You may find a highly negative child will respond to kindness or cheer with pouting. Some very positive children are capable of remaining pleasant when surrounded by nastiness.

However, we usually get back in like kind. In the long run, even the negative child will show the world the tolerance you showed her. You may not see this at home, while she is young. Because children have not yet learned to curb their natural first reactions, they tend to react in ways adults do not. For example, have we not all cringed as a child asked a physically challenged person what happened to their eyes, or why they cannot walk? This candor is a normal part of being a child, and does not reflect poorly on parents. Temperament-based social blunders are the same sort of thing. These embarrassing moments simply mean the child has not yet learned to modify natural responses over which she has little control. An attempt to change temperament-based behaviors with severe or swift consequences will not work. You will strain your relationship with your child with such tactics . . . and your relationship is the cornerstone of your ability to teach.

Tips to Remember

1. The first step in improving family relationships is to focus on the strengths of each member's temperament.
2. *Model* the behavior you wish to see in your children because example is the most effective teaching tool.
3. Respect your children's true selves.

Seven

Building Good Family Relationships

Childhood is a very short part of the overall life span of a family, yet often it sets the tone for the next forty or fifty years. What would you like your adult-to-adult relationship to be with your children? You can start now to develop it. This investment in the future will also make the present more enjoyable.

Some parents feel guilty because they like their "easy" child better than their "difficult" one, thinking that they should love both the same. But, we all respond differently to different behaviors.

Probably, like most of us, you too feel good when you interact with an easy child and not so good with one who rubs you the wrong way. The easy child lets you think you are a pretty good parent, while the child who causes you difficulties makes you suspect you are less than competent.

You may have conflicts with your spouse over the challenging child, but agree over the easy one. Other people may criticize you for the behavior of your challenging child, but never make a point over anything the easy child does. Emotions such as embarrassment, anger, resentment, and exasperation may describe your relationship with the hard-to-manage child, while feelings of pride, warmth, comfort, and companionship accompany interactions with the easy child. Any normal human would have a preference for pleasure versus pain.

Take a look at how this natural human favoring plays out in some families. There are lots of possible scenarios; here are a few typical ones. Mom feels guilty about her negative feelings towards the challenging child. So, she compensates for her favoritism by indulging that child. Mom has inadvertently rewarded poor behavior, so the child repeats it. Perhaps Dad spends more time with the easy child, and the difficult one acts out more to get his attention. Sometimes the easy child takes on the role of the parent's partner and confidante, especially in a single-parent household, as the frustrated parent turns to him or her for support.

You can avoid such complicated problems as shown above by being open and honest and remaining clear that while you love both children, some behaviors are more pleasant to be around than others.

Focus on Behavior

Let your easy child know that you appreciate his many wonderful qualities. Let your challenging child know you appreciate her many wonderful qualities, as well. Describe the behaviors you enjoy and like to be around. Avoid falling into the over-simplified trap of "good boy/bad girl." Talk very specifically about what you like in their behavior, and what you do not like, so the children can identify how it is they are getting the reactions they get.

People who dislike a child's company when he or she is obnoxious give great feedback—if they let the child know exactly what drove them away. Likewise, unless parents specify which behaviors they enjoy, the easy child may get the message that he is somehow superior in character to his sibling, when, in fact, his temperament simply harmonizes with his parents' and his environment.

Neither child is trying to be "good" or "bad." Neither is "better" or "worse" than the other. They are just behaving according to temperament. Give yourself permission to have whatever feelings you have about each child. Congratulate yourself for continuing to improve your parenting skills. As you accept your feelings, know that you can have them while behaving differently than you usually do. Get on with strengthening the relationships you have with your children. Start from wherever you are, and build for the future.

Take Care of the Easy Child

Beware that you do not overlook the easy child in your relationship-building efforts. The idea is that you enhance each relationship, helping it grow from the level of closeness you have now, to a new level. If you already have a close relationship with an easy child, you will go ahead and nurture it. If your relationship with your challenging child is poor, you will start there, and work to improve it, too, but not to the exclusion of others. Certainly, too many parents have essentially abandoned easy children while they focused all of their parenting energy on a challenging sibling. One of the biggest drawbacks to being an easy kid is that you look so okay nobody pays you much attention. In this way, easy kids can get lost in the shuffle, and their needs can go unmet.

One mother realized that she and her husband spend an enormous amount of time, money, and attention on their challenging son. They constantly try to channel his high intensity and high activity in positive ways, which is a good thing. For them, the valuable discovery was this: they rarely do anything extra for their easy daughter! They made a conscious decision to start balancing resources a bit more, and to do some extra things for the overlooked child. This is wise, since it stops any resentments the easy child may have been harboring and prevents future problems. It also ensures that the easy child has the opportunity and encouragement to learn new things, too.

Self-talk Helps You Cope

Some parents who are trying to stop struggling with a challenging child develop self-soothing mantras to repeat at the time the child is really getting to them. They say things like, "She's flooded with feelings she can't control," or, "He's reacting according to temperament," or, "Life is hard for her in many ways," or, "This is real to him," or, "I can stand apart from this." Our favorites are: "I'll laugh about this in the morning," and "This won't matter ten years from now." You can also do some deep breathing, counting, or leave and take a walk someplace else away from the child if it is safe to leave him.

As you step back and disengage emotionally, you make space for new responses to old behaviors. In the new space, a stronger relationship can grow.

For easy children, your self-talk might be simply "Where is my easy child right now? What does he need at this moment? Have I focused my attention where I am most useful?" Remember that sometimes you can accomplish two goals at once. Simply turn away from the misbehaving child and focus your attention on the behaving child. This act simultaneously tells the children that you like the positive behavior and dislike the negative behavior. If your habitual reaction to one child's acting out is to address it directly, you may feel odd when you turn away. If you feel angry, it may seem insincere to offer kind praise to the child who is not pitching a fit.

For example, if Sarah is reading a book and Sophie is having a temper tantrum, you can say, "Sarah, I love the way you are reading. May I join you? Let's go someplace quiet where you can show me your book." Then you and Sarah move away from Sophie and pay no attention to her. Be aware that the acting-out child may respond by trying harder to get your attention back. You will need to resist the temptation to attend to her demands. You may feel considerable stress as you pay attention to the behaving child and ignore the other's behavior. That is okay. You can continue to feel the old feelings and still do something new. After all, that is what you are asking your kids to do.

Fifteen Things You Can Do to Build Close Relationships

- **Be together.** Find little bits of time to relax together. During this time, you are not going to act like a parent, but more like a friend.

- **Get away from home.** Often, familiar patterns trigger habitual behavior between people. If you go to a different place, those behaviors are stopped because the familiar patterns are broken up.

- **Step outside your authoritarian role as parent.** For certain bits of time, consciously stop correcting, instructing, advising, etc.

- **Play together.** This can be hard if you have forgotten how to play. Just go ahead and follow the child's lead. Swing, climb a tree, share toys, enter into his imaginative games, dance (sway, move, march) to music. Go ahead and be silly together.

- **Reverse roles.** Let the child teach you something. Ask questions. If you do not know how to play "Barbies," ask the child to show you. Honor her expertise.

- **Have a conversation.** Ask the child what she thinks about different things. Get her to feel comfortable really talking to you. Forget about telling her what you think, unless she asks you. Listen closely.

- **Distance yourself.** If things have gotten really bad, split up for a while to cool off. This may mean you go away for a while, or the child does. Then come back together and see if you both feel different. It is far better to send your child to your mother's for a week than to abuse her. There is no shame in taking a long break. While you are apart, think of one or two things you plan to do differently to improve your relationship when you are back together .

- **Share a special activity.** Find something you and your child both love, and do it together. Just the two of you. Consider establishing a tradition.

- **Make one-to-one time.** Relationships, to be intimate, do not include groups of folks all the time. They are "just you and me" things. This means excluding other family members sometimes. When other people are not influencing the two of you, your interactions become simpler.

- **Reveal yourself.** Share things about yourself that you have never told your child. Let him know you are a human being with feelings much like his. This may come as a surprise to him. Tell stories about your own childhood, or about your own parents when you were young.

- **Admit when you are wrong and make amends to your child to repair the damage.** You will not become a doormat if you do this thoughtfully. It is wonderful modeling for the child, who may one day be able to tell you she was wrong and would like to make amends to you.

- **Enjoy special confidences.** Certainly we need to share important concerns with our spouses, but for older children, intimacy means that you will not tell everything she shares. Likewise, you must be willing to allow her to have special confidences with others without expressing jealousy. We cannot control our gut reactions. We can control our expression of them. This is a powerful way of honoring your child.

- **Accept your child as he is, at this moment, flaws and all.** Tell him he is okay, and believe it. Talk about changes as if they are about "getting better and better," not about becoming acceptable. Acceptance of the child is the key to a healthy relationship.

- **Tell your child, "I love you."** Encourage touching. If hugs are not acceptable any longer, leaning or sitting close together might take their place.

- **Enlist support of your spouse.** Talk with your partner about steps you are both willing to take to build your relationship with your child. What can you do to support one another in this? Perhaps you will volunteer to take turns with the other kids for an afternoon, so that one of you can have one-to-one time with a child. Maybe you will agree that buying tickets to an event as a treat for one child is a good use of money, and you can do something special for the other kids another time. Whatever you come up with, do it.

Tips to Remember

1. Concentrate on developing and maintaining positive relationships with your children. This activity will take time and energy!
2. Be clear with your children about the *behaviors* you like and do not like.
3. Be careful during stressful times that you remember to pay attention to your easy child.

Eight

Environment and Goodness of Fit

The fit between your child and her surroundings can have a great deal to do with whether she is able to meet the demands of that environment, or not. For example, if a highly irregular child is born into a household where both parents work variable shifts, that child probably will have no problem adjusting. On the other hand, a very regular child would have a terrible time with the constant disruptions in schedule. Similarly, a very high activity child born in a large city with severely restricted opportunities for outside play will likely have trouble. A low intensity, low activity child may thrive in the same setting. Sometimes, the environment itself is the problem. While moving to the suburbs—or the farm—might not be possible for the apartment dweller with the active child, joining a club might be.

A child whose temperament profile showed high activity, irregularity, intensity, and distractibility came to my attention. I knew nothing about this family and visualized a very challenging child. I anticipated a very frustrated parent, but, to my surprise, the mother reported that this was a great kid and they had no problems! The family lives on a large farm where there are lots of opportunities for activity and exercise and commotion. The wonderful fit between the child and his environment probably prevented many problems that would have occurred in a more restricted environment.

The complexities of environment and temperament fit are immense. Try to assess your present living situation in terms of your child's unique style. What parts fit? What parts do not? Can you make adaptations to improve the fit?

Parents' Temperaments

Another big piece in goodness of fit is the temperamental makeup of the people in your child's life. You are probably the most important person in your child's life. Therefore, it is wise to assess your own temperament in order to learn how your style fits with your child's style. You might also want to consider the temperaments of your spouse or partner, your day care provider, siblings in the home, or others with whom your child spends significant amounts of time.

The easiest combinations of temperaments are among people who fall in the mid-range on the temperament trait scales. The most volatile interactions between people occur when they are either very much alike or very much different. People with a lot of high and low scores tend to be quite challenging. When they are with others who also tend toward extremes, the group can end up in conflict.

If you and your child are both very intense, a lot of theatrics may be going on. You play off of one another's intensity, escalating already intense emotion. If a quick-to-approach parent has a slow-to-approach child, he will feel exasperated with the child much quicker than the parent who is himself shy. A distractible child and a distractible mother together can really irritate a persistent father who is locked in on completing a task. He cannot understand why his child and his wife are off doing six other things! The opportunities for various interactions among family members are endless and fascinating.

We can examine complex interactions according to the temperament traits that drive them. One mother shared that on her honeymoon her new husband became furious with her when she happily leapt onto a wide, stone bridge railing overlooking a deep, rocky canyon. She danced along this precipice admiring the view, which horrified and then angered her husband, who imagined her falling several hundred feet to her death. Because of his intensity, he expressed his fear and anger very emotionally. Because of her high approach and positive mood, she never for a moment considered falling, and was mystified by his reaction.

In the first chapter of this book, you took a look at your child's temperamental make-up. In the next few pages you can assess your own temperament, then compare your child and yourself. You can also compare your temperament to your partner's, or to that of other children. It can be very helpful to ask your own parents, or others who knew you when you were very young, to give you insight as to how you were as a small child. Assessing adult temperament can be tricky, since we have spent many years learning to modify reactions that have brought us disapproval. The older we get, the more this socialization obscures our natural first inclinations. Therefore, looking only at your adult selves will not necessarily give you a true picture of your temperament.

Activity

Your overall preference for active or inactive play; your overall energy level throughout the day.

Best clue: Leaving television and movies aside and disregarding "shoulds" about exercise, how would you fill your leisure time? In activity or relaxation? Would you be "on the go" or idle?

Low activity   **High activity**
Calm and slow moving   **Wild and quick moving**

|_____|_____|_____|_____|_____|_____|_____|

Adaptability

How easily you adjust to attempts by others to influence what you are doing or thinking.

Best clue: Do you adapt quickly to changes, new places, ideas, expectations? Is it difficult or easy for you when there is a new routine or schedule?

Fast adapting   **Slow adapting**
Easygoing   **Strong willed**

|_____|_____|_____|_____|_____|_____|_____|

Approach

Your initial tendency for responding to a new experience such as meeting a new person, tasting a new food, being in a new situation. (Disregard learned social conventions.)

Best clue: What is your first and usual reaction to new people, situations, or places?

Quick to approach   **Slow to approach**
Outgoing   **Slow to warm up**

|_____|_____|_____|_____|_____|_____|_____|

Distractibility

How easily your thought processes or attention are interrupted by things going on around you.

Best clue: Are you very aware and easily diverted by noises and people? Do you get sidetracked from what you said when something else catches your attention? Can you distract yourself from upset feelings by redirecting your attention?

Low distractibility
Not easily diverted

High distractibility
Easily diverted

Emotional Sensitivity

The ease or difficulty with which you respond emotionally to a situation. This trait has two sub-scales, one for sensitivity to your own feelings and your sensitivity to others' feelings.

Best clue: Do you often become upset "over nothing," or do you rarely become upset even when circumstances suggest that you could? Do you feel sympathy for or empathy with others acutely?

Self

Insensitive to own feelings
Unaware of emotions

Highly sensitive
Feels own emotions strongly

Others

Insensitive to others' feelings
Emotionally tuned out

Highly sensitive
Emotionally tuned in

Intensity

The amount of energy you commonly use to express emotions.

Best clue: How physically dramatic, fierce, or passionate are you when expressing strong feeling? Do others find you easy or hard to "read?"

Low intensity
Mild reactions

High intensity
Dramatic reactions

Mood

The amount of pleasant, friendly perception and behavior as contrasted with unpleasant and unfriendly perception and behavior.

Best clue: Is your usual first response to new ideas "No!" or "Yes!" Are you an optimist or a pessimist? Light-hearted or serious?

Positive mood   **Negative mood**
Generally carefree   **Serious, displeased**

Persistence

The length of time you will continue to make an effort, especially when the task gets hard or boring.

Best clue: Do you stick with things even when frustrated? Can you easily stop an activity when asked to?

High persistence   **Low persistence**
Get "locked in"   **Stop easily**

Regularity

The day-to-day predictability of hunger, sleep, and elimination. Consider each function separately and rate it on its own scale.

Best clue: Do you normally tend to go to bed, wake up, or want your meals at the same time each day?

Hunger

Want food at same time   **Irregular eater**

Sleep

Tired on schedule   **No schedule**

Sensory Awareness

How sensitive you are in each of these sensory channels: 1) pain, 2) touch, 3) taste, 4) smell, 5) hearing, and 6) sight. Rate each channel on a separate scale.

Best clue: How aware of noises, temperature changes, lights, odors, flavors, and textures are you? How do you respond to pain? It is possible to be very aware in some channels and unaware in others.

Pain

"What nail in my foot?"   **"EEEEEEEOOOOWWW!"**

Light touch

No reaction to contact   **Easily irritated or pleased**

Taste

Can't tell the difference   **Notice tiny variations**

Smell

Don't notice odors   **Human bloodhound**

Hearing/Sound

Don't notice noise   **Sensitive to sounds**

Sight/Light

Visually insensitive   **Visually sensitive**

Now that you have assessed your child's and your own temperaments, you can take a look at the ways you and your child fit well and do not fit so well. You can also explore the fit you and your spouse share, which is interesting, too! As you compare your temperament with that of your child, you may better understand what goes on between you. You may have already noticed that there are certain times when you will clash and other times when you will get along beautifully. You may even be able to predict situations in which problems, or no problems, will arise. Predicting will help you plan the situations in which you put yourself and your child. This planning will help you enjoy more conflict-free activities while avoiding anticipated problems.

Susie, a slow-to-adapt child, who was invited to a Halloween party. Susie and her best friend decided to go as "twins." The costumes were carefully planned in advance. The day of the party, Susie called her friend to check on a detail, and learned, to her utter dismay, that the friend had changed her mind and was going as an astronaut! Susie was devastated. To her, this change meant that she could not go to the party, since she could no longer go as planned as a twin. Susie's low adaptability made it difficult for her to imagine a different costume. Her older sister helped her figure out a new costume. She refused to put it on. Instead, she went to the party (taking the costume along, just in case) and asked the hostess if she could come without a costume. The hostess said she could, so she wore her regular clothes. What a difficult time Susie had because of her low adaptability! As a result of this experience, her mother learned that Susie needed help planning for the unexpected so that she could avoid such crises in the future.

Challenges to Temperament Create Stress

Combinations of traits within the same person lead to interesting behavior. A child with very high intensity and low approach came home from school very upset about something that had happened during the day in her fourth grade classroom. She was telling her story to her mother with great feeling, crying and gesturing, in a loud and dramatic voice. The phone rang, and to her mother's surprise, the child answered it in a controlled, normal tone of voice. This shows how even high intensity people can shut down when they feel compelled to approach slowly. This child's temperament traits were acting in opposition at that moment, and slow approach won out over intensity, as it had done all day at school. Imagine the effort the child had exerted to hold in this torrent of feeling until she got home and could freely express her intensity in a safe place. In this example, one trait actually challenged the other, creating stress for the girl.

Stress comes from "challenging a trait." To challenge a trait is to create a demand contrary to the person's temperament. In Susie's case with her Halloween costume, a slow-to-adapt child was challenged by an unexpected change in plans. You could challenge a distractible child by putting her in a room full of commotion and giving her a deadline on a task that takes all of her concentration to complete. Sometimes you will choose to challenge a trait in order to teach new skills, or "stretch" the child. It is through these challenges that we all learn new ways of coping.

At other times, however, you may wish to avoid challenging a trait. You might choose not to challenge a trait in order to keep the peace. If there is little to be gained by the challenge, or the added stress would pose a hardship for everybody, skip it. For instance, if you are attending the county fair with family and friends, this may not be the time to ask your high activity child to practice slowing down. It might be better to pair him with his equally high activity, but older and wiser cousin, and turn them loose to enjoy the rides in their own breakneck style. If you are low intensity and low activity, be somewhere else doing something you like, because you will not enjoy the shrieking and rampaging of these perfectly normal children.

Lots of situations will naturally challenge your traits as well as your child's traits. When either of you is experiencing a trait challenge, there will be stress. When both of you are, the stress doubles.

You can predict likely stressors, and then choose when you want more or less stress by manipulating the circumstances into which you put yourself.

For example, if your child is very active and very intense, you may be asking for trouble to expect him to sit quietly through a religious service. Imagine how you would feel if you were a low activity and highly emotionally sensitive person. You would be able to sit through the service, and you would also be aware of the annoyance others feel at your son's inappropriate behavior. You might then feel intensely embarrassed, self-conscious, and angry. You can see how different combinations of traits, within one person or two people who are interacting, can produce unpleasant experiences.

Avoid Stress

Look at the results of your temperament analysis. Start by identifying traits in which you scored at either extreme end of the possible range. We call these extremes "core traits," and they are very important. For yourself and for your child, jot down a list of core traits. Whenever you and your child share a core trait, circle it on the list. Now take a moment to think about what these differences and similarities mean about how you get along.

Discuss with your spouse or think over what situations will likely result in positive interactions, and what situations will likely cause negative interactions between you. For example, a mother and son with opposite moods see things very differently. The mother predicts that when her son is bemoaning the doom and gloom he finds all around him, she will have a hard time being patient with his outlook, since she does not share it. The slow-to-approach father of a quick-to-approach daughter may view her as socially forward, based on his own hesitance to meet new people. On the other hand, a quick-to-approach parent may feel frustrated by a slow-to-approach child who refuses to take part in games at a party. An adaptable parent who must ask a slow-to-adapt child to switch plans at the last moment will feel quite put out by the child's resistance. A family full of slow-to-adapt people, each with a pre-conceived idea of how things are going to be, may have tension or conflict even during play time.

There will also be opportunities to maximize the good times, based on core traits. If you have, for example, a low activity, emotionally sensitive, and not very distractible child, and you share those traits, the two of you will probably have a wonderful time at a long, sentimental theatrical production. Two highly regular people will get along fine at camp where the day runs on a tight schedule. If both the parent and the child are highly persistent, staying with a project a long time will feel natural to both of them, and they will probably work well together.

Sometimes there are situations in which opposites create a good experience for both or for one person. For example, one mother said she gets carried away by her own positive mood. She is grateful to have a less positive child who can always point out the risks involved in some new scheme she has. What sorts of things do you enjoy with your child, based on temperament? What would be difficult for you to enjoy together?

Imagine yourselves at each of these activities: a baseball game, the research library, a funny movie, a funeral, a chess tournament, a visit to your great-grandmother in a home for the elderly, the circus, and a fancy restaurant. What goes on at each location? What environmental demands does the event itself pose? In which places will you be likely not to have problems with your child? Which situations will likely create trait challenges and stress?

When you understand the temperaments in your family, you can decide which activities will provide the most pleasure and the least stress for all. When you plan accordingly, you are not "spoiling" your family, you are avoiding problems and building positive relationships.

Ways to Change the Environment to Fit Your Child

CHILD IS/SHOWS:	YOU CAN DO THIS:
Low activity	• Encourage active pastimes: roller blading, dog walking, hiking and camping, swimming, gardening, etc. • Provide interesting, calm pastimes: games, musical instruments, books, crafts, etc.
High activity	• Provide calm activities: board games, cards, movies, crafts • Acquire sturdy furniture • Lock up sharp objects, tools, and poisonous substances • Provide large muscle activities: trampolines, swings, bars, trikes and bikes, outdoor chores, etc.
Fast adapting	• Give ample supervision and teach safety rules
Slow adapting	• Keep transitions to a minimum • Make few changes to who lives in your house and which bedrooms they have • Keep furniture in the same place
Quick to approach	• Put away breakables • Give ample supervision • Lock up dangerous substances • Accept messes
Slow to approach	• Ask people your child does not know to pay little attention to child

CHILD IS/SHOWS:	YOU CAN DO THIS:
	• Keep child in same school as long as possible
	• Keep same care givers as long as possible
High distractibility	• Limit visual and auditory stimulation when child needs to concentrate or go to sleep
	• Rotate toys to decrease quantity available at one time
Low distractibility	• Nothing special needed
Emotionally insensitive	• Utilize media to show portrayal of emotions, especially empathy and caring for others
Emotionally sensitive	• Monitor media that may be scary or overwhelming
High intensity	• Be an audience for theatrical performances
	• Listen to your child
	• Soundproof if you live in an apartment
Low intensity	• Nothing special needed
Positive mood	• Nothing special needed
Negative mood	• Provide pleasant influences through books, music, etc.

CHILD IS/SHOWS:	YOU CAN DO THIS:
High regularity	• Keep a predictable schedule for meals, sleep, and activities
Low regularity	• Accommodate this child's unpredictability and flexibility • Minimize unpleasant objects and activities
High sensory awareness	• Cut tags out of clothes; avoid scratchy clothes • Buy seamless socks • Reduce overall volume of sound in home • Keep home at comfortable temperature
Low sensory awareness	• Teach child to become aware through art, music, cooking, etc. activities

Tips to Remember

1. Your child's environment has two parts: the physical one of place and the emotional one of his parents' temperaments.
2. Challenges are most likely between people when they are very much alike *or* very much different.
3. Carefully assessing your own temperament will lay the groundwork for you to understand and improve your relationship with your child.

Nine

How to Help Children Adapt Their Behavior

Effective discipline always means not wasting precious energy on minor problems. There are times, however, when you need to help your child behave more appropriately.

Most of us cannot focus on more than three behaviors at a time without feeling frazzled. If your household has many children, one behavior per child may be plenty to think about. To sort out truly significant behaviors from the merely annoying, ask yourself: Is it life-threatening? Will it matter in five years? Is it a temperament-based behavior that will not change unless we work on adapting it? Is it a new behavior? Can we live with it for a while? Might it go away by itself?

Put lower priority behaviors on hold. *Cultivate the ability to ignore, an invaluable skill for all parents, especially overwhelmed ones.*

Wait and See

You can use the "Wait and see" technique for lots of small, irritating things. Stuff like baby talk, muddy shoes, the occasional bad word, spills, teasing, forgetfulness, getting home a little late, splashing water, not cleaning the plate, forgetting to flush, doing a chore imperfectly, leaving lights on, losing things sometimes, making a rude comment, or not replacing the toilet paper roll are all examples of things you can live with for a while. The list is endless. Many of these behaviors are related to development, not temperament, and will take care of themselves in due time if you do not make a big deal out of them.

To use "Wait and see," you say nothing about the issue, but watch to see what happens. You appear to be ignoring, because you make no response to the child. You are actually tracking carefully, while you just as carefully refrain from reacting. You simply go on about your business while silently observing. For example, when your child says a bad word, ignore it. See if it happens again. It may not. Ignoring is especially useful for behaviors related to developmental growth, such as spilling, having accidents while toilet training, telling tall tales, or using language oddly. These types of things will usually go away by themselves as the child matures.

Ignoring is also helpful if a harmless but annoying behavior is being used to seek attention inappropriately. Interrupting, for example, may sometimes be eliminated by ignoring. Go right on with your conversation, ignoring the interruption. The child may stop if interrupting does not work.

If the child does not stop the behavior after a reasonable amount of time, you can still ignore it while redirecting or distracting him. Refocus his attention elsewhere without mentioning the annoying behavior: "Jason, would you take your pillow and sleeping bag to your room, please?" or, "Look, Aunt Susie is handing out Popsicles!"

Avoid showing disapproval of the behavior, since doing so clearly shows you noticed. If you have trouble ignoring, leave the room, involve yourself in a new activity, or pay attention to a child who is behaving well. You may discover that you have been reacting to all sorts of little things, using priceless energy on trivial issues. It may come as a great relief to learn that you can let many things go and actually improve your own energy level and your effectiveness in matters that really make a difference.

Sometimes parents say it is a challenge to act calm when they are seething inside. And, sure, it is. At first, you may need to "act." As you do this, you will probably notice that your emotions begin to match up with your chosen response. As you act kind and patient and wise, you will begin to feel kinder and more patient and wiser inside, too.

Talk with your spouse or think over which things you can call minor annoyances. Consider ignoring them. One therapist colleague of mine tells parents that it is the job of kids to drive their parents a little crazy (that is how they find out what behavior is appropriate and what is not). So when the kids are annoying you, simply note that they are doing their job. Decide which behaviors you are choosing to "Wait and see" about.

Recognize Your Child

Sometimes parents fear that giving children too much recognition will spoil them. Have we not all heard that compliments will go to their heads, making them arrogant, conceited, and hard to live with? This is a common notion, but there is not much evidence that compliments really work that way. Over-indulgence and exaggerated or insincere praise are not helpful to children. Used sensibly, however, gifts and kind words will not spoil your child. On the contrary, a child who has the chance to earn rewards learns a valuable lesson. A child who believes he is lovable and capable behaves more positively than one who does not. When you encourage your child with recognition for desirable behavior, you provide the incentive for him to repeat the behavior. We human beings all respond this way to recognition, and children are no exception.

Recognition comes in many forms. Things we see and touch

provide long-lasting recognition, but words are excellent, too. "Bragging" on your child, money or tokens, praise, or a get-together celebration can all provide recognition. Oddly, negative attention such as a reprimand or punishment also provides recognition. In this way, we sometimes accidentally encourage behavior we would like to stop.

Keep in mind that *whatever you attend to you will get more of!* It does not matter what kind of attention you pay to the behavior, because all attention is reinforcing. For this reason, ignoring is a powerful response to minor problems. Remember the vicious cycle? This principle explains something about how the vicious cycle is kept in motion. The child misbehaves, gets a big reaction, and misbehaves again. The solution is to start paying more attention to the child's positive behaviors and less to the negative ones.

I have noticed that rare families exist which have actually managed to create the opposite of vicious cycles. These families seem to enjoy a self-perpetuating cycle fueled by approval, appreciation, and recognition. While most of us did not grow up in one of these super-positive families, we can learn from them if we choose to.

Consider your family's style of giving recognition. Some families are reserved with their recognition. In these families, gifts, cards, and special foods are given only on holidays and birthdays. If you come from a reserved family yourself, it may seem odd, unnecessary, or even a bit embarrassing to imagine celebrating small successes. You may feel that small achievements are "no big deal." Cooperation, you may feel, is simply expected, not rewarded. If you were reared this way, you are not alone.

Other families are very free with their recognition. They celebrate often, creating moments which acknowledge one another for even little achievements. Bringing a C grade up to a B, cleaning out the garage, or going to the dentist without a fuss might all be cause for recognition of some sort. By giving recognition, they tell each other, "I know that wasn't easy for you, and I'm proud that you did it!" Silly as it might seem to some people, they may go out for ice cream because Billy remembered to take his lunch to school.

Make a Fuss Over Your Child

Families who make a "big deal" out of small successes end up having kids who really want to achieve and who put energy into behaving well. Low intensity families and high intensity families will create different ways of making a big deal out of a small success. Regardless of the form it takes, we all love recognition, even if it seems corny. Try it. Your child will eat it up. So will your spouse. They may roll their eyes and shake their heads, but they will be grinning! Recognition feels good. That is why it is a huge motivator, a powerful parenting tool. Ask any camp director what makes camp so special. She or he will tell you it has to do with the creation of lots and lots of opportunities for gaining recognition and receiving it through some manner of group ritual. Kids thrive on it.

Now is a good time to think about the atmosphere of recognition in your home. How easy, or hard, is it to get recognition? Both positive and negative events are occurring all the time in all homes. Ask yourself, what do we focus on most? What do we emphasize by the amount of attention we pay the events? Are we playing up the negatives or the positives?

Someone once said that it is not the amount of bad things in your life that determines its quality, rather, it is the amount of good things. If this is so, we have a large measure of control over our own happiness. While we may not be able to eliminate bad things, we can almost always include more good ones. The same is true for our children's lives, and recognition is something good we can always add.

Ways to Offer Recognition

Some ways to recognize your child as a valuable person include: making verbal affirmations, commenting on accomplishments, recognizing helpful actions, hanging artwork, looking over school papers, and attending school conferences. Children feel recognized when you go to their athletic events, concerts, plays, speeches, or awards ceremonies. Likewise, you can honor your child by arranging transportation to events, having her friends over, or acknowledging a report card. Knowing her likes and dislikes and accommodating them when you can is powerful recognition. Most of these activities do not cost much money; they do cost a bit of your time, though.

One powerful form of recognition is a celebration. Good celebrations have several different elements, and families that repeat the same sorts of things end up creating a family ritual. This is a good thing. Your family may have already established some traditions of its own. If not, and you would like to try it, incorporate some combination of these elements: talking about the success; giving a small, symbolic gift; making a special meal; baking a cake or other goodies; singing a song together; giving flowers; presenting a card, special letter, certificate, or poster; lighting a candle; giving special thanks during grace or bedtime prayers; taking and displaying photos; going to a favorite restaurant together.

When you plan a celebration, take care that what you plan fits the temperament of the person you want to honor. For example, one new step-mother organized a surprise party for her daughter. This child was slow to adapt and tended to withdraw, not approach. For her, an unexpected, large group of people, some of whom she barely knew, leaping out at her from behind the furniture was a nightmare. When celebrating, try not to challenge a trait because people do not feel honored by that experience.

The experience of being honored far outweighs the value of the tokens representing the recognition. You need not spend a lot of money for recognition to be powerful. Take a few minutes now to reflect on how you presently celebrate. What events do you recognize? How do you show your appreciation? Do you want to expand on this? What could you realistically add? Remember that words are very powerful and they are free and readily available.

Tips to Remember

1. Your job as parent will be much easier when you ignore behavior that really does not matter in the long run.
2. Change your child's behavior and improve the atmosphere in your home by practicing "Wait and See" and "Recognize Your Child."
3. Recognize your child by saying and doing things that take temperament into consideration.

Ten

Out with Labels,
In with Descriptions

T he language we use in our relationships with other people
affects how we see them, sometimes in subtle ways we are not
aware of. Use of critical labels that tell a child she is unlovable
or incapable affect our behavior toward her in negative ways. Getting rid of these labels is another way to focus on positive behaviors
and downplay negative ones.

Think for a moment about the effect of language on your child
and on yourself. What happens when a critical description of a
behavior "sticks?" When a child is called a "brat" several times a
day, over time he begins to believe he is a brat and the chances of
him behaving badly increase accordingly.

Martha is a highly distractible child who was in trouble a lot
until her parents learned about temperament. Martha and her

brothers all had chores to do around their home. Martha's brothers did not have much trouble getting their chores done promptly, but Martha had a terrible time. Her mother would tell her to go feed the rabbits and on the way to the rabbit hutch she would see something, anything. It could be a marble. So she would stop to pick up the marble and look at it, and in that instant, she forgot all about the rabbits. She would walk around outside looking at her marble while her mother, watching her from the window, fumed about how lazy and unreliable she was. Children like Martha are often accused of being "passive aggressive," of dawdling, and of deliberately making others finish their tasks or wait for them. Martha actually is quite energetic and willing, traits her parents can see now that they have renamed laziness and unreliability as distractibility.

Sometimes children are misunderstood when two or more traits are creating tension inside them. This kind of stress comes from having traits that actually pull us in different directions at once. Have you ever found yourself caught between two traits? It is easy to call yourself some uncomplimentary names at these times. It is easy to label your child, too, when such a circumstance occurs.

Two temperament combinations in which the traits oppose one another are high approach and low adaptability, and high distractibility and high persistence. High approach says, "Go for it!" while low adaptability says, "Wait a minute!" High distractibility says, "Oh, I must do that, too!" then high persistence takes a turn and adds, "I've just got to finish this now, even if it is 3 a.m.!" It is easy to become critical at times like these. Negative words cut away at healthy self-esteem (the belief that we are both lovable and capable) in adults and children.

The Power of Labels

A description rapidly becomes a definition of who the person is. This is true of all name calling. If you want to begin to dislike an individual, call him an ugly name. When you label a child in a negative way, you and everyone else see the child as bad and hopeless. Getting to a neutral description from a negative one will help you start to think and feel differently about the child. It can also help prevent harmful, self-fulfilling prophecies.

By about age six, a child can begin to understand simple information about his own temperament. He can begin to learn language for talking and thinking about his temperament. Andrew, at about age eight, announced in response to a new idea, "You know I'm slow to adapt. Give me some time and then let's talk about it." This child had not only learned about himself, but about advocating for his needs. His own insight provided relief to his family because he spared them from his initial first response, which almost surely would have been negative.

Teaching a child about himself in this way will help him manage his responses later, and may help him feel better about himself now. A challenging child is often the target of name calling. However, hearing an explanation of how others sometimes see him can help him cope, especially if the explanation is restated in neutral terms.

"Positive" Labels Are Harmful

We sometimes label easy children with positive terms that do not truly identify the pleasing quality that is being praised. An easy child may mistakenly believe he holds the moral high ground, when actually it is his low intensity and high persistence people appreciate. Changing "he's such a good little worker" to "he can really stick with a job a long time" may seem like a very small change, but the comment is now more specific, and tells the child how he is a good worker. Likewise, calling a child a "sweetheart" seems harmless, but it might mean more to the child if you told her what she did that pleased you. Tell her, for example, that you really liked the way she tuned in to your feelings and showed that she cares. When you point out her emotional sensitivity with your praise, you help her understand more about herself. While the self-fulfilling prophecy in a complimentary label is usually better than that of an uncomplimentary label, it would be best to avoid labeling kids altogether, and instead teach them what pleases and displeases us.

An easy child may be getting more credit than he has coming, while a difficult one may be getting less. When you understand that most behavior is temperament based, you can see how this works: neither child is attempting to be "good" or "bad." Each is simply being himself, according to the dictates of his temperament. To judge one "good" because he is fortunate enough to please us and to judge the other "bad" because he is unfortunate enough to irritate us is a disservice to both kids. In truth, all temperaments have both pleasing and displeasing aspects, and much of the determination is in the eye of the beholder.

Give Specific Information

Try simply to make a comment based on what you observe about your child's traits. This gives the child specific information and makes praise more meaningful. Use neutral, descriptive language that reduces the temptation to name call. It helps you be more understanding and patient with the child. Step back from those behaviors that really bother you. Instead of saying that an intense child is a screamer or hysterical, note that he certainly is emphatic or enthusiastic. An irregular child might be called erratic or contrary. Replace labels with a simple observation like, "She often isn't hungry or sleepy when others are." You can comment that a slow-to-approach child takes time to get used to new places, rather than labeling him shy, aloof, or clingy. Saying a child likes to do things her own way, or has a lot of determination, is less critical than calling her stubborn or pig-headed. A child with a high activity level can be said to have great energy, get revved up, or move quickly and often. Refrain from calling her a maniac, wild woman, or ape.

In the same way, describe a child who feels things acutely as sensitive and kindhearted, not sweet or nice. We can describe one who finishes tasks as having great perseverance, not as a little beaver. We might describe one who is reserved as quiet or soft-spoken, not as a little lady or gentleman. We can say a child who is adaptable makes changes easily, rather than referring to her as a regular trooper.

Whenever you change a label by turning it into a brief description of the child's temperament, you change the way you see the behavior, and you do the child a favor. Instead of attributing behavior to the label ("She's doing that because she's a quitter; he's acting that way because he's a prince."), you can attribute it to a trait. This may at first seem like splitting hairs, and you may think, what is the difference? There may even be some truth to the label–low persistence people *do* quit. What is the harm in calling a spade, a spade?

There is a huge difference! Negative labels describe people in a critical way and readily become put-downs. Positive labels describe people in a flattering way, and readily become false or imprecise praise. Negative labels, repeated often enough, poison your opinion of your child as well as his opinion of himself. Positive labels, repeated often enough, inflate your child with empty words and saccharine-coat his opinion of himself without substance. If you want to value your child, affirm that she is capable and lovable by giving specific, descriptive praise. She needs evidence that what you say is true. If you want to invite your child to try new ways of behaving, give her specific, descriptive feedback on what it is you want to see more of. Both negative labels and empty praise keep people stuck. Replacing them with descriptive statements is a powerful step in putting language to work for you.

Change a Label to a Description

To see a behavior differently, start by identifying the label you have used in the past. Then ask yourself what trait is most likely driving the behavior you are seeing. Next, make a simple, understanding statement that describes the behavior. Look for neutral terms that tell what is happening. When you describe undesirable behaviors, avoid words that imply this is always the way it is, or that change is very difficult, unlikely, or impossible. Skip words like *can't, hard, trouble, tough, impossible, never*. Strive for neutral, factual descriptions. An excellent description is kind, positively stated, and either offers genuine praise or gently invites growth and change while acknowledging challenges.

Here are some more examples of labels changed to descriptive phrases based on temperament knowledge:

Label: That little monkey! Look at her bounce off the walls!
Description: Right now she's getting wound up. It's sure a challenge for her to quiet down.

Label: He's such a goldbrick. He won't do his chores.
Description: He gets overwhelmed when he has too many jobs to do all at once.

Label: He's always been such a cry-baby.
Description: Sometimes he feels things so deeply he cries.

Label: She's mama's helper.
Description: She is energetic and sees what needs to be done.

Label: He's a shrinking violet.
Description: He needs some time to get used to strangers.

Label: She's such a sweet girl.
Description: She is sensitive to others' feelings and shows she cares about them.

Avoid labels and instead describe what you see to your child, and to all children. If you are describing an undesirable behavior, the shift will set the tone for joining with the child to make needed changes. If you are commenting on a desirable behavior, you will be offering sincere praise which recognizes and reinforces specific behavior. Descriptions of your child help her feel understood, and

Common Labels Translated into Temperament Descriptions

LABEL	TEMPERAMENT TYPE
Goofball, clown	High intensity, high approach, high activity, low emotional sensitivity
Crybaby	High emotional sensitivity, high intensity
Wallflower	Low approach, high emotional sensitivity
Wet blanket, spoilsport	Low adaptability, negative mood
Eager beaver, go getter	High approach, high activity, high adaptability, positive mood
Nerd	Low activity, high persistence, low distractibility, low emotional sensitivity
Know-it-all	High persistence, low emotional sensitivity, high intensity, low adaptability
Space cadet, air head	High distractibility, low persistence, low sensory awareness
Brat, curmudgeon	Low adaptability, negative mood
Holy terror, life of the party	High activity, high intensity, high persistence, high approach
Sweetheart	High emotional sensitivity, high adaptability, positive mood

teach her about herself. She will better understand her own temperament.

You can begin to educate family and friends who may still be labeling instead of describing by using descriptions with them. If the look on your mother's face says, "What a stubborn kid!" you can say, "It's a challenge for Robbie to shift gears and change activities." Whether you restate a positive or negative label, your descriptive statement changes the matter from one of character to one of behavior.

Realistic Self-Understanding

All parents want to raise emotionally healthy children. This means teaching them what is good about their inherent nature, along with what might need some modification. Children begin to think poorly of themselves if the adults around them view their qualities as bad. It is easy to call a shy child "chicken." It is easy to call a caring, cooperative child a "princess," especially if she is attractive. Neither label is an accurate depiction of the child. Seek to describe traits in neutral terms, and to point out how each trait may be appropriate at various times.

Convey to the child that he has a wide repertoire of behaviors, and this is good. If you keep referring to the shy child as "careful," it gives him an alternative to accepting the "chicken" label. If you name the compliant child cooperative or easy to get along with, it will be more meaningful than the label "princess." The goal, of course, is to help the child develop a healthy, but realistic sense of self. The more positive you are about your child's temperament, the more positive he will learn to feel about himself.

Temperament and Teens

Your child's teen years are an especially good time to talk with her about temperament issues. This is the time when peer pressure is most powerful, and your child is very vulnerable. Your teen is faced with many, many temptations when she joins her friends away from your protection. Fortunately, at this age she can also understand what temperament is and how it works. With your help she can grow to understand herself. As she grows in self-understanding, she will become clearer and clearer about who she is, how she reacts to new experiences, and what she will and will not do. This clarity will help her resist temptations and maintain healthy self-esteem—the knowledge that she is both capable and lovable.

For a child with a challenging temperament, the teen years can be hard times. If others neither understand nor accept his temperament, they may do or say hurtful things, things that end up making him feel that he is a bad person. You can take this opportunity to teach him ways of dealing with a world that will not always be kind to him. Support him by becoming his champion, but more importantly, teach him to stand up for himself. Teach him how to ask for what he needs, based on his knowledge of himself.

The 19-year-old daughter in a family I know is becoming an expert at self-advocacy. She is mastering the skill of asking for what she needs without sounding like she is making excuses for herself. Her parents shared their assessment of her temperament with her. Now that she understands how her high activity level, high distractibility, and low persistence play out in various life situations, she is often able to plan so that these traits are accommodated when reasonable. For example, before a two-day seminar, she told the instructor that she needs to take periodic breaks and would sit at the back of the room so that she could leave and return without disturbing people. Since she feels calmer and stays more focused when her hands are busy, she takes her knitting for the long stretches of lecture time. She is learning to manage the challenging aspects of her own temperament.

For an easy child, adolescence may hold problems, too. One drawback for positive mood, approaching, adaptable kids is their increased vulnerability. They trust everyone and they go along with whatever is happening. Up to now, in the sheltered environment of your home, with your friends and trusted associates, this has been fine. In fact, it has been more than fine. It has been a joy. Now, with increased freedom comes the risk of getting involved in dangerous activities or with untrustworthy people. It is not only rebellious kids who say "yes" to risky endeavors—it is sometimes also the highly adaptable, highly approaching, optimistic kids. The needed skill is how to exercise caution and skepticism. The 15-year-old daughter of a friend of mine wisely noted, "So, like, I thought about how I *am* and everything—you know, like really, really social, like practically a party animal—and I decided I'd better think this through like I was someone else, you know, like I was someone that thinks before they just, like, go off!" She was able to decline an attractive invitation to a party with several college boys by understanding her own temperament and working to curb her natural first impulse. Not only could she make herself safe, she was able to talk with her parents about the experience.

Talk with your teenager about how different situations have affected her. Talk about feelings together, and how others might perceive her because of her temperament traits. Help her to see herself through the eyes of someone who does not appreciate temperament as you do. Such candid talks may suggest ways the teen wants to change a little. Your tolerance and acceptance will build her self-esteem and help her cope with criticism from others.

Tips to Remember

1. Neutral descriptions of *behavior* help you think and feel better about your child.
2. Develop a rich vocabulary to aid you in changing from labels to interesting and accurate descriptions of your child's behavior.
3. Take advantage of a teen's intense interest in self-understanding to help him or her cope with pressures to do unsafe or undesirable things.

Eleven

Discipline or Punishment? An Important Choice

Sometimes parents feel that they must use punishment or they are not doing their job of raising compliant children. Pressure can come from any number of well-meaning sources, from in-laws to religious leaders and even school staff. In my professional and personal experience, punishment is usually ineffective. It is not a necessary component of effective parenting.

While most parents expect professionals to discourage corporal punishment, many continue to administer it as though it could actually "teach a lesson." In fact, it does not teach the lessons the punitive parent intends to convey. Punishment may temporarily stop an undesirable behavior or push the behavior underground where you will not see it anymore. Worse yet, punishment refocuses attention away from the error and toward the person giving the punishment. Who was ever sent to their room to "think about what you did" who spent the time contemplating their mistakes? If you were like most children, you sat fuming about the unfairness of it all. Perhaps you even planned revenge. You certainly thought angry thoughts toward the person who made you go to your room.

Similarly, a child who is spanked, say, for hitting her brother, does not think "I'd better not hit anymore," but rather, "I sure won't let Dad see me do that again." In this case, we see the absurdity of hitting to extinguish hitting, which cannot work because modeling is so powerful a means of teaching behaviors.

Origins of Punishment

Historically, the law has held a man responsible for the actions of his wife and his children, as well as for damages caused by any animals he owned. Because of this liability, he was given free rein in controlling those in his charge. Children were to be seen and not heard. They were on earth to serve and to please their parents to whom they were expected to be subservient, dutiful, and grateful. Unfortunately, this absolute power often led to abuse of women, children, and animals. The predominantly European-based culture in the United States comes from a tradition of stern child-rearing methods. It has been, until quite recently, perfectly acceptable for parents to use whatever means they deemed necessary to control children, who were viewed as wild and untamed creatures by nature. Beating a child, like beating a woman or an animal, was not considered a bad thing, since fear was an effective method of control.

While I am sure most parents today do not believe as our ancestors did, some attitudes left over from those days are still with us. Let us take a look at punishment, and contrast it with good discipline, so that you can decide for yourself how important punishment is in your repertoire of parenting skills. There are many good, effective parents who believe in it, and many who do not.

Before we go on, however, I want to offer a word of warning. Some parents, especially those who grew up abused, or who are high intensity, high activity people, or who carry a lot of anger, have found that it is not a good idea for them to spank. They realize that the spanking is more for their own satisfaction than for the child's benefit, and they also know they can get carried away and overdo it. To avoid this, they wisely choose not to spank or inflict other forms of physical punishment.

One father told me, "I can't afford to use corporal punishment with the kids or to get physical with my wife. It's not that I don't want to hit 'em. Sometimes I really do want to. It's that if I do, I turn into the man who raised me. It's diabolical, and makes no sense. I hated what he did, and there I am doing the same things to the people I love the most! I used to swear if I ever had a wife and kids, I wouldn't treat 'em like he treated us. But it's so easy to slip into." This man used his self-awareness to safeguard his family. He became a fine husband, parent, and manager at a residential center for delinquent youth. His challenge was to find safe ways to discipline all the children under his care.

Discipline Versus Punishment

Now, to compare punishment and discipline. According to the dictionary, punishment consists of: a penalty imposed on an offender for a crime or wrongdoing; to cause to undergo pain, loss, or suffering for a crime or wrongdoing; to treat harshly or injuriously; generally connotes retribution rather than correction. The goals of punishment are to regain control, establish your authority, force compliance, and stop unwanted behaviors. The means of punishment are physical force, verbal hostility, humiliation, extreme deprivation, and emotional abandonment. Punishment can stop unwanted behavior for the short run, but it also encourages revenge and sneakiness. Forcing children does nothing to teach them respect, but rather conveys that in conflict, the more powerful person will win. Overpowering a child does not help him develop conscience. Punishment focuses the child's attention on feelings of anger or hurt, which cause him to forget what he did wrong.

Punishment may clear the air. It may lead to making up and showing affection, and it provides a release for the parent's anger and aggression. It is also quick and easy. In the long run, however, it teaches very little of value and *simply does not work* to achieve the results you really want.

The dictionary definition of discipline includes: a branch of knowledge or learning; training that develops self-control, character or orderliness, and efficiency; training which results in self-control or orderly conduct; practices to be imparted to disciples. Discipline's goals are to teach socially acceptable behavior; to teach children to solve problems and make good choices; to develop conscience; to encourage self-discipline; to enhance self-esteem; to establish limits and teach children to live with the consequences of their actions.

The means of *discipline* are less familiar to most of us than those of punishment. They are also more difficult to carry out. They require effort, planning, and time. To discipline, you:

- **Communicate assertively.** Say directly and plainly what you want: "Stop teasing Johnny NOW."

- **Reinforce good behavior.** Verbally reward the behavior by saying something encouraging about it: "I'm so proud when I see you sharing with Johnny."

- **Allow natural consequences and encourage your child.** Let whatever is going to happen take place without interfering, as long as it will not be unsafe. Then say something that expresses your hope for the child to do better next time: "I'm sorry you had to walk to school today. I'll bet tomorrow you are on time for the bus."

- **Impose a logical consequence.** Relate the consequence directly to the misbehavior: "Since you didn't stop squirting water as I asked, I'm taking away the squirt guns and you must go to your room to calm down."

- **Involve yourself with your child's life.** Find a way to join in with your child so you learn about his experience of the world. A parent who volunteers to co-lead her child's play group learns firsthand about problems her child is having.

- **Be patient and consistent.** Remain calm and stay with the same house rules: "I know you don't want to go to bed right now, but nevertheless, nine o'clock is bedtime around here, and we will stick with it."

- **Set an example.** Let your child see you solve a problem without violence and disagree without name-calling or belittling.

- **Practice desired behaviors.** Create and use strategies for learning new skills, the cornerstone of good discipline, since we form habits out of repetition.

The consequences of discipline are that children learn to respect you and other people. They develop conscience, morality, responsibility, and self-respect. They develop *self-discipline*. They feel good about themselves, and the bond between you and them is strengthened. They learn to trust.

If You Feel You Must Punish

Punishment is especially ineffective for temperament-based problems because it usually sets the vicious cycle in motion. If, however, you are very sure the behavior is not temperament based, it is *very* serious, and you feel you must punish, keep these guidelines in mind: be clear about expectations and consequences. The

Comparing Punishment with Discipline

CHILD'S BEHAVIOR	PUNISHMENT
Dawdles, is slow to get ready (Low adaptability)	Assign extra chores, nag and lecture, spank
Hits cat or dog (Quick to approach and high activity)	Slap hand, spank
Runs into street (Quick to approach and high distractibility)	Spank, scream threats
Swears (All traits)	Wash mouth out with soap
Steals from store (Quick to approach)	Spank, threaten, criticize; ground to room or home for several weeks

and the Use of Natural Consequences

DISCIPLINE	NATURAL CONSEQUENCE
Help child get up earlier; reward child each time she catches school bus.	Child misses bus, has to walk to school and deal with being late.
State, "Do not hit the cat. Stroke gently like this." Show child how to pet animals.	Child gets scratched or bit; animals avoid her and do not want to play.
Strongly state, "It is very dangerous to run into the street. Do not do it. Stop at the curb [edge of yard, etc.]." Show child the boundary you wish him to observe and practice running up to it and *stopping*. Increase close supervision of child to prevent harm.	*No natural consequence is safe—cannot use!*
Wait to see if behavior continues. Use a star chart to reinforce appropriate language.	Other adults express disapproval to child.
Take child to store and have him return or pay for item he took. Teach him words to use to apologize to storekeeper. Stay with him and support him while he makes amends.	Child is banned from the store, cited by police.

child needs to know what things will be punished. Explain simply, "You may not run into the street. If I see you do it, you will go to your room." Let the punishment be symbolic. The ritual is more important than the punishment itself. Being grounded is more important than the length of the grounding. Punish only for behavior. Be clear that you do not like what she did, but you do like her.

Forget about motives. Do not bother demanding to know why they did something. Kids rarely know why they did something, or they know exactly why and so do you. They rarely do things to "get you," even though it sometimes seems that way. Be brief. Do not explain at great length. Say simply, "You played with matches and that is not allowed. Now you are having the consequence." That is plenty. Do not negotiate. Make the rules clear, then punish without warning and without discussion. Do not nag or threaten. Be firm. Sound neither apologetic nor angry. Stay neutral and do not act out of your anger. Be serious and mean business. A new problem behavior deserves one warning, "It is NOT okay to color on the wall. If you do it again you will be punished." Last of all, do not harm your child with any punishment.

Some nonphysical forms of punishment include: grounding; restriction from television, telephone, or computer; removal of privileges; assignment of extra chores; or time-out. Whatever you use, be sure it is something you can enforce. For example, if the child will talk on the phone while you are away, you may need to put the phone in your purse when you leave the house (but be sure the child has some way to get emergency help if she needs it). If you give extra chores, first be sure you have a child who will actually do them, otherwise you have set up a power struggle you cannot win.

You will have to decide for yourself where you stand on the question of punishment and discipline. Sort out what kinds of misbehavior you wish to punish and what kinds you wish to discipline. Reserve punishment, if you choose to use it, for very serious behaviors.

Tips to Remember

1. Punishment is not a necessary, or effective, tool for raising capable, lovable children.

2. Genuine discipline requires effort, planning, and time. Spend time teaching your child what you want him or her to know.

3. If at times you choose to punish instead of discipline, reserve it for very serious behaviors and do no physical or emotional harm to your child.

Twelve

How to Prevent
Temperament-based Problems

The better you understand your child's temperament, the easier it will be for you to predict problems before they happen and to avoid them. This understanding will also help you identify needed behaviors and devise ways of teaching them. For a challenging child, knowledge of temperament is essential. For an easy child, it will help you pick up on subtle problem areas that may be very important, but which can go unnoticed. Easy kids pose a different set of concerns for parents. Part of what makes children challenging is that they are "in your face" with their stuff. You cannot miss it. Their misbehavior is so bothersome that it demands attention. With an easy child, you can miss a lot that is going on right in front of you. This is especially true if there is also a challenging sibling who commands your attention.

For example, your low approach, low intensity, easily adaptable, and highly persistent child may be struggling to master math facts. Unfortunately, no one knows this because he never asks for help, expresses his frustration, or gives up. How would you know he has been repeating errors over and over? You will be even less likely to notice this if your challenging child is in the midst of a crisis and has all of your attention.

As you think about grouping behaviors into clusters according to temperament, be sure to think about your easy child as well as your challenging one. While your easy child's problems may seem minimal, you can improve the healthy development of every child by using these techniques. To start, think in terms of typical behaviors. Use whatever words come to mind to describe the behavior, even if (for the moment) it is a label. Certain types of behavior tend to indicate various temperament styles.

For example, really picky, hard to please or finicky behavior usually comes from high sensory awareness and perhaps regularity. One girl nearly drove her parents crazy with her constant critiques of foods. By age twenty-one, however, she had become a highly paid, world-traveling coffee buyer. Her exceptionally astute sense of taste was the cause of both great frustration in her family and great success in a specialty field of work. She turned a liability in to an asset.

BEHAVIOR GROUP A

The Child Who Is Difficult to Manage

- Ignoring, contrariness, and defiance come from low adaptability, pessimistic mood, and high persistence.
- Stubbornness, having to have his own way, and refusing to accept "No" come from low adaptability, high persistence, and sometimes from regularity or irregularity of biological needs.
- Shyness, timidity, holding back, and face-hiding are earmarks of emotional sensitivity and slow approach.

Note: Although these traits seem undesirable, they have protective qualities. Persistence pays off in the long run. If a person really needs to support a position, refusing to budge can be an asset. Slow-to-approach folks seldom regret hasty decisions because they do not make them.

BEHAVIOR GROUP B

The Child Who Is Difficult to Keep Healthy and Safe

- Too trusting or gullible behavior stems from quick approach and optimistic mood.
- Risk-taking and dare-devilish behavior can come from high activity level and optimistic mood.
- Competitiveness can arise out of high persistence, high activity level, and high intensity.
- Being too obedient and following others mindlessly comes from high adaptability and optimistic mood.
- Not taking things seriously, being nonchalant, or flippant sometimes come from low emotional sensitivity, optimistic mood, and low intensity.

Note: Giving away possessions, not sticking up for one's self when bullied, and other non-assertive behavior comes from a combination of several traits. Most commonly, they include: low intensity, high adaptability, optimistic mood, low persistence, low activity level, and high emotional sensitivity to others' feelings.

BEHAVIOR GROUP C

The Child Who Is Difficult to Be Around

- Complaining generally comes from pessimistic mood, low adaptability, and high sensory awareness.

    Imagine a little boy who sees things as worse than they are, who takes a long time to adjust to changes, and who picks up on subtle differences. Now imagine that his parents are moving to a strange new town. Can you understand his homesickness, his need to complain? He will be very slow to adjust.

BEHAVIOR GROUP D

The Child Whose Attitude Is Difficult to Tolerate

- Interrupting is driven by quick approach, high activity, high persistence, and low distractibility.
- Rudeness can come from high activity, quick approach, and high intensity coupled with low emotional sensitivity to others' feelings.

Note: Imagine yourself very wound up, fearless, energetic, and "locked in" on an issue. Your high persistence and low distractibility cause you to get stuck. If you are also intense, that is, you express yourself dramatically, you may interrupt non-stop until you are satisfied. Learning to wait, interject ideas, or change the subject appropriately will be a challenge for you!

BEHAVIOR GROUP E

The Child Who Has Difficulty Focusing

- Wild, excitable behavior usually comes from high activity, high persistence, high sensory awareness, quick approach, and high intensity.
- Forgetfulness flows from high distractibility and low persistence.
- Silliness can come from high distractibility, high intensity, and high activity level. Some children cannot complete the simplest tasks because they always wind up somewhere else.
- Physical aggression is found in kids with high emotional sensitivity to their own feelings and/or low emotional sensitivity to other's feelings. It is exacerbated by high intensity, high activity, and high approach.

Take a moment and identify a few clusters of behaviors that concern you, then determine what temperament trait is likely to be behind the behavior. You may need to refer to the temperament chart you prepared for your child. You may get stuck. Not every behavior is clearly temperament based. Temper tantrums, for example, seem to be universal to childhood. Temperament will determine *how* the child expresses a tantrum, but not whether he will have a tantrum or not. Procrastination, jealousy, attachment and bonding, manipulation and goal-seeking seem to cut across all temperaments, rather than typify one or two. If you are the lucky parent of easy children, you are really fine-tuning now. If you are working with a challenging child, determining the temperament trait behind the behavior can be a matter of survival for you.

Remember, when you can predict, you can plan. A parent who is surprised by nothing can deal with just about anything. By understanding your child's temperament well, you will be able to say to yourself, "I knew this would happen." You will not fall prey to disbelief, outrage, and indignation, all of which will surely undermine your cool. *Your cool is your biggest asset in reducing strong reactions to misbehavior.* As you calm your reactions, you gain self-control. As you gain self-control, you improve the odds that you will be effective when you step in to change things.

When you identify clusters of behavior, think about when and where the behavior is most likely to happen. Make an estimate of how often it happens. Consider with whom it happens most. Put related behaviors together. Identify the trait behind the clusters. This is a picture of your child in action. Become thoroughly familiar with it. It is the basis for creating management strategies that fit your unique child.

What to Do When Skills Are Missing

Parents occasionally comment that their children seem really savvy at some times and really oblivious at others. They cannot figure out why a kid would be smart one minute and dumb the next. This may not be a matter of smart or dumb, or of common sense failing in certain circumstances. In temperament terms, your child's natural first reaction may simply be very appropriate in certain situations. In other situations, his natural first reaction may simply be entirely inappropriate. In both cases, the reactions are coincidentally appropriate or inappropriate. Your child is neither trying to be "good" nor "naughty." He's just being himself, according to his temperament. Where his behavior is appropriate, there is a good fit. Where it is inappropriate, there is a bad fit. Chances are, once he knows what behavior you want and receives recognition for good performances, he will try to please you.

All children need to learn some skills that, due to temperament, do not come easily to them. Each of the ten traits suggests both talents and missing skills in children who strongly exhibit the trait. Children can be missing many trait-based skills. When you begin to manage according to temperament, knowing what you want to teach is essential. Here are some commonly needed skills and their related traits.

Strengths and Needed Skills by Trait

TRAIT	STRENGTH	NEEDS TO LEARN TO:
Activity		
High	Is energetic	Release energy appropriately
Low	Can be still physically	Exercise enough to be healthy
Adaptability		
High	Is flexible	Think independently
Low	Holds strong convictions	Consider other ideas and options
Approach		
Quick	Meets people easily	Apply caution
Slow	Is naturally cautious	Take risks when reasonably safe
Distractibility		
High	Notices everything	Focus attention
Low	Focuses	Shift focus more easily
Emotional Sensitivity		
High	Understands on a "feeling" level	Maintain perspective
Low	Expresses emotions clearly	Care and be concerned
Intensity		
High	Feels everything passionately	Regulate passionate energy
Low	Is calm	Express emotions clearly
Mood		
Optimistic	Sees the bright side	Discern unpleasant reality
Pessimistic	Sees the dark side	Relax and have fun
Persistence		
High	Has tenacity	Let go when appropriate
Low	Figures out easier ways to do things	Stick with tasks

TRAIT	STRENGTH	NEEDS TO LEARN TO:
Regularity		
High	Predictable body functions	Create lifestyle that fits body rhythms
Low	Not bound by clock time	Adhere to clock time when necessary
Sensory Awareness		
High	Is alert or sensitive to environment	Ask for or find accommodations for sensitivities
Low	Is tolerant; unaware	Be aware in order to detect danger

Weaknesses and Needed Skills by Trait

TRAIT	WEAKNESS	NEEDS TO LEARN TO:
Activity		
High	Has difficulty sitting still or relaxing	Pace self to others and to situation
Low	Is unfit	Get enough exercise for health
Adaptability		
High	Is easily influenced	Use good judgment
Low	Wants to do things his way	Consider other options
Approach		
Quick	Engages in risky behaviors	Control impulses and consider consequences
Slow	Is shy	Learn social skills
Distractibility		
High	Is easily sidetracked	Maintain focus
Low	Does not notice what's going on	Be aware and shift focus

TRAIT	WEAKNESS	NEEDS TO LEARN TO:
Emotional Sensitivity		
High	Has trouble being analytical	Keep emotions in perspective
Low	Can be unresponsive	Be empathetic
Intensity		
High	Overwhelms others	Regulate emotional energy
Low	Can be misunderstood	Express emotions
Mood		
Optimistic	Does not take things seriously	Recognize when people or situations are serious
Pessimistic	Takes things too seriously	"Lighten up"
Persistence		
High	Continues beyond what is reasonable	Know when to quit
Low	Takes longer to learn skills; doesn't like practice	Stick with things
Regularity		
High	Can be "run" by food and sleep needs	Schedule for biological needs
Low	Has trouble adjusting to others' schedules	Take responsibility for eating and sleeping on own schedule
Sensory Awareness		
High	Is preoccupied with sensory influence	Adapt environment to sensory needs
Low	Does not notice sensory influence	Adapt environment to compensate for obliviousness

As you begin to think about the skills your child needs most to master, refer to his or her temperament chart and consider the core traits (the extremes) you identified earlier. These areas will probably be the most important to focus on. You will probably have no trouble identifying missing skills for a challenging child! It is a bit trickier to find what is missing for an easy child. Use your knowledge of your child as you jot down several skills he or she would benefit from mastering.

Tips to Remember

1. Make your job easier by identifying clusters of behavior problems and the temperament trait(s) responsible for them.
2. Pick *one* strength at a time and help your child learn a needed skill associated with it.
3. Pick *one* weakness at a time and help your child learn a needed skill associated with it.

Thirteen

How to Deal
with Problem Behavior

So, you have read 95 pages now and your child is still misbehaving? In this chapter, you will learn different responses to undesirable behaviors and practice becoming confident at selecting and using the new responses. Be very patient with yourself. Habitual patterns are often so well learned that they are automatic. Doing something different takes planning and effort, but will pay off in the long run.

There are several choices you can make, according to the situation you are in at the time your child misbehaves. Here are *five actions* you can choose from when you notice a problem. Select the right action for the situation.

1. **Rescue.** This is the action you must take in a life-threatening emergency. *Do whatever you must to protect your child.* When you are both calm, use the experience as an opportunity to teach the skill your child is missing.

2. **Impose consequences.** This is the action you take for rule violations. Breaking rules calls for consequences and then teaching. State the rule and the consequence. Do not lecture. Follow through. Later, teach again why the rule is important.

3. **Wait and see.** Some problems are related to development and will pass in time. To use this action, you stop, think, and observe. Do not respond to the behavior. Redirect or distract the child, leave the area, or purposely attend to something or someone else. Use this action for minor problem behaviors.

4. **Do as little as possible.** Use this action when you are so fatigued, ill, stressed out, or rushed that you cannot deal effectively with the misbehavior right now. Do the least you can do to bring the situation to an end. Use no more words than necessary. Postpone any other action. There will be other opportunities for dealing with this problem later when you can do so effectively.

5. **Teach skills.** For the long term, you will want to develop management strategies. Use these to teach needed skills. You will learn how to create your own management strategies in the next chapter.

Action Chart

You may want to post copies of this "Action Chart" around the house for quick reference until you learn the choices by heart.

- **Rescue!**
1. Is the child's behavior life-threatening?
2. Protect your child NOW.
3. Later, teach what to do differently.

- **Impose consequences.**
1. Did the child break a rule?
2. State the rule and the consequence for breaking it.
3. Follow through with the consequence.

- **Wait and see.**
1. Is this a minor problem?
2. Stop, think, observe.
3. Ignore the behavior as long as it remains minor.

- **Do as little as possible.**
1. Are you ill, tired, stressed out, or rushed?
2. Do as little as is necessary to bring the situation under control.
3. Wait for a more convenient time to teach new skills.

- **Teach skills.**
1. Do you wish to deal with temperament-based behavior effectively for the long term?
2. Think about what you want the child to learn.
3. Create or select a management strategy to help your child learn how to change a temperament-based behavior.

Mentally Rehearse the Actions

In order to use these actions effectively, you need to become comfortable with them and confident that they will work for you. Mentally practicing the choices will prepare you to use them successfully. To start, do not worry about changing what you are doing. At this point, the most important changes are going on inside your head. You are going to learn how to break the process of responding to behavior into small steps so that you can learn more easily.

Your task for now is to begin to think differently. Once the new thinking starts to feel comfortable, you can try to discipline differently. For now, a few more days of old behavior is better than becoming overwhelmed. Do not put energy into changing both your thinking and your actions at once.

The only thing you need to do differently right now is wait ten seconds as you run through the various actions you can take. First, glance at the "Action Chart." Familiarize yourself with the five actions, and go over the steps in using each one. Do this until you feel comfortable and confident with each action. Take your time. Some parents take several weeks to rehearse alternative actions before they have a sense of mastery. Talk with your spouse about how the process feels to you. Remind yourself that change takes time.

One of the biggest challenges is to break a behavior pattern that we have practiced again and again over months or years of parenting. Old responses have become automatic. They are rapidly triggered by thoughts and feelings that occur when we see behavior we do not like. The responses become almost reflexive. The *ten-second pause* is the technique for stopping the reflexive response and replacing it with a thoughtful response.

Another reason to rehearse is that you want to use your new actions gracefully. You want to select and use your actions smoothly, like a skilled traffic cop who knows quickly which hand gesture is needed to direct the mass of autos after a ball game. This requires repeating the new steps over and over until they, instead of your old response, become automatic.

Imagine several scenarios with your child and talk your way through them, selecting the best action for each situation. You may be surprised by how quickly you can search the action chart mentally for the best action. Take all the time you need to mentally rehearse. When you feel confident, begin to use the actions with your child. Go through these three steps each time your child misbehaves:

1. Is the behavior life-threatening? If so, rescue. If not, go to Step 2.
2. Stop, take ten seconds to calm yourself.
3. Select the best action from the five on the Action Chart and use it. If it does not work, choose a different action.

Sometimes parents report something interesting happens about this time. They notice their child's behavior is changing. She or he is acting better. How could this be, so soon? The answer has to do with the vicious cycle. Mental rehearsal helps you become less emotional when you respond. Simply taking the ten-second break and thinking can calm your reaction so that even old ways of disciplining feel different to the child. Consequently, the cycle is interrupted. This does not always happen. Your child may misbehave as before. It may take a little longer to disrupt the cycle. Expect delay! Be persistent.

Pick Three Behaviors to Work On

With your spouse or partner, go over the behavior clusters on page 93-96. Ask yourselves, which behaviors are causing this family the most trouble? What bothers us the most? Which behaviors create the most difficulty for our child? Which behaviors, if resolved, might reduce the overall stress level in our home?

If a certain behavior seems fairly distressing and fairly easy to manage, put it at the top of your list. Anything you can do quickly and easily that will make a difference is worth doing first. Now narrow down your list to the top three behaviors. These are *all* you attend to for starters. You and your partner should agree to work on these issues; let the others go for now, and support one another in your efforts.

Two more techniques can help you prepare to use your new system for discipline. It is normal to get all ready to start and lose confidence. If you do not feel ready, try reinforcing what you already know with imagery or role playing.

Imagery

Imagery is a proven practice method used by athletes and others to enhance performance. It can work for you. The beauty of imagery is that it removes you from the heat of the moment so you can concentrate. When you are alone, quiet, and have a few free minutes, sit or lie down and make yourself comfortable. Relax. Breathe deeply. Let the cares of the day drain away. Now imagine a large, white movie screen. You are the writer, producer, and director of the scene. You will soon be an actor, too, in the unfolding drama. Next, picture an episode in which your child is being very challenging. Imagine this in 3-dimensional, Technicolor with wraparound stereo sound. Make the scene vivid. Maintain your calm, relaxed state. This should be easy since the misbehavior is imaginary, not really happening. Now, you, the master parent, enter the scene. Imagine that you are mentally going through the steps of selecting the best action. If you have not already done so, take a few moments to try this now, referring to the Action Chart on page 104 as needed.

Watch yourself using your new actions with grace, elegance, and composure. See what it feels like to be in control, thinking calmly and clearly. Picture yourself succeeding. You are cool, thoughtful, and effective. Nothing surprises you or throws you off your new path. You sense the new response becoming second nature as you practice it. If you are a visual learner, picturing your-self in the scene is a powerful way to master information. Such mastery will allow you to recreate the scene in real life. Repeat this exercise as many times as you like until you carry the confidence with you into a real-life scene.

Role Playing

Role playing is the second way to practice. It also removes you from the urgency and intensity of the moment and lets you think. It is faster paced than imagery, which is okay because it helps you *practice* at a quicker pace, something you will need to be able to do when you start working with your child.

Find a willing partner to play your misbehaving child. With your partner, establish a setting. Determine where you are, who is there, and so on. Your partner gets to choose one of the three prob-lem behaviors you have decided to start with, and then acts it out. Someone who has seen your child in action can stay in character best. His or her job is to try to surprise or shock you while remain-ing true to your child's temperament.

Your job is to be unshockable while talking yourself through the steps of choosing and using the best actions for the situation. As your partner goes on playing your child, you begin checking the actions on your chart. Talk right out loud, but to yourself. Your "child" cannot hear you; in real life, your talking would happen inside your head. When you have selected the best action, you approach your "child." At this point, he or she can hear and respond to you.

You have five actions from which to choose. Go ahead and play out scenes using actions one through four. If you choose the fifth action, you cannot play through yet. You have not yet learned any management strategies because they are in the next chapter, so sim-ply say, "Now we are going to use a strategy," and end the role play. Soon, when you have some strategies, you can role play using them as well.

When you have progressed, try role playing without your action chart handy. You might also begin talking to yourself silently instead of aloud. You may find that role playing injects humor into what can become a deadly serious business. Laughing at your problems is a wonderful way to lessen their power over you. When the problem has less power over you, you will learn faster and gain confidence more easily.

How to Role Play in Five Easy Steps

1. Select a behavior that you wish to change.
2. Act out a scene in which this behavior occurs, with your spouse or some other partner playing your child.
3. Act out the scene again, using one of the actions you have chosen to help you. (See page 104 for the steps to follow for the action you have chosen.)
4. Talk about the scene with your partner. Will the action you chose be likely to work with your real child? Would you like to try again with a different action?
5. Make up new scenes and practice using the actions until you can use them automatically. Now you are ready to work with your child.

If you need to, and your partner is willing, you can role play as many different situations as you can think up. An added bonus of doing this with a partner is that you can talk about the process as you experience it. Some of us are highly verbal and learn best when we hear information. Others of us are kinesthetic learners and need to move around while we learn. Role playing allows for these different kinds of learning. Play out the whole scene, and then talk about it with your partner afterwards.

There is another benefit to enlisting a partner in the role playing. Critical people can become allies once they understand what you are trying to do. Even if they do not totally agree, they will respect you when they see how hard you are trying! To people with no knowledge of the five actions, it can look like you are "doing nothing" while you stand back and mentally go through the options.

Having a partner play your child and then reversing roles opens up all kinds of opportunities for discussion and for building a cooperative relationship. Imagine how great it would feel to find yourself in a real-life situation similar to one you role played, and see your partner give you a wink and a thumbs up sign! If you are both "in" on it, he or she might support you that way–or at least not say, "Are you just going to stand there while he does that?"

This is hard work. Ask for help when you need it. Take a break when you are tired. It is all right to get help from any willing adult. When you feel that your confidence level and expertise with the actions are good enough, not perfect, you are ready to start learning about management strategies.

Tips to Remember

1. Five different actions give you great power in solving behavior problems: 1) rescue, 2) impose consequences, 3) wait and see, 4) do as little as possible, and 5) teach skills.
2. Practice using the actions mentally and in role playing before you use them with your child.
3. Along with your spouse or partner, pick no more than three behavior problems to work on at any one time and take action.

Fourteen

Behavior Management
Strategies for Living

Management strategies are the form of positive discipline I recommend for seventy-five percent of problem behaviors. They are designed to teach a certain skill, related to a problem behavior which has a clear temperament origin. Not every idea for teaching children is a management strategy. *The management strategies are specific to temperament traits.*

Here are several underlying assumptions of the temperament approach to parenting. These are essential to know if you are to use management strategies well. For the most part, your child wants to learn to behave acceptably and to please you. You want to teach and guide your child peacefully. There is no one more qualified or motivated to do the job than you. Anger and frustration may get in the way, blinding us to the first and second truths above. Punishment may appear to stop negative behavior, but it does not, by itself, promote positive behavior. To work best, a method of discipline should take into account both the problem at hand and the innate characteristics of the misbehaving child.

Honoring preferences is not "spoiling" your child. It is a way to "work smarter, not harder." Children and parents want to have close, loving relationships that include mutual respect for individual differences. Children and parents both win when they convert a combative relationship into a cooperative one. In such a winning relationship, the parent is mentor, teacher, coach, and sometimes benevolent dictator. The child is a creative learner. Regardless of what approach they use, parents *will* put enormous energy and effort into rearing children. Since there is no getting around it, putting this effort into planning and teaching makes more sense than putting it into continuing the vicious cycle. Unlike relationships with friends or co-workers, relationships with our children are lifelong ones. Therefore, it is worth the effort to make them good.

Management strategies are experiences you use to teach your child skills that do not come naturally to her. The strategies can be simple or complex. You can do some on the spur of the moment. Others take props, materials, or further planning. Remember that what works for one child may not work for another, and what works today may not work next week. Human growth is dynamic. The trick is to keep experimenting to find what works for you. Here are three strategies as examples. They address common problems.

"Look at Me"

Problem: Not listening, ignoring

Temperament trait: High distractibility

Description of behavior: "I understand it's easy for you to be drawn away."

Needed skill: Ability to focus and hold full attention

What to do: Parents of distractible children often say their child "won't listen." The word "won't" implies that the child is doing this on purpose. Remind yourself that the child's temperament causes him to be drawn away by small distractions. Replace your hurt and anger with love and sympathy. Say to yourself, "This is my distractible child." Say to him, "Now look at me and listen to what I have to say." Say it gently and firmly, while looking him right in the eye (or whatever is appropriate for your culture). Saying it angrily will defeat the purpose.

Then ask him to repeat back to you what you told him. You can suggest this to his teacher for use at school, too. You can also ask that he sit in the front row where he can have frequent eye contact with the teacher without seeing thirty kids between himself and the teacher. Thirty kids provide all kinds of distractions!

"Inside Voice, Outside Voice"

Problem: Loud voice or rowdy behavior

Temperament trait: High intensity

Description of behavior: "I understand it is natural for you to like to make noise."

Needed skill: Control over volume

What to do: This strategy helps your dynamic, intense child to learn to regulate her voice. You tell her you are going to play a new game. Then you take her on an adventure to practice inside and outside voices. Make a list of places to visit. Just before you get to each place, talk about which voice is to be used. The inside voice is quiet and respectful of other people. Model the volume for her. The outside voice is as loud as you want it to be, as long as you do not disturb people. Model this, too. Your child needs to practice using each voice. Have fun together. Keep playing the game for several days. Continue to talk about appropriateness as you go to different places. Good places to include on your list might be libraries, parks, swimming pools, the river, a hospital, the mall, Grandma's house, school, place of worship, a fair, the zoo, or a country road. When your child has mastered a wide variety of voice levels and the game is over, you can cue her by using what you taught. Say, "Too loud. Time to switch to your inside voice." This feedback will help the child learn to monitor herself.

"Break Time"

Problem: Restlessness
Temperament trait: High activity, high distractibility, low persistence
Description of behavior: "I can see you are getting restless and uncomfortable."
Needed skill: To learn a socially acceptable outlet for tension, to refresh attentiveness.
What to do: Getting fidgety and losing concentration go with this temperament territory. So, assign a short, distracting activity: "How about taking a break to help me set the table?" Encourage the child to return to the original task in a few minutes. In school, the teacher can have her erase the blackboard, carry a note to another teacher, or go get a drink of water. At home, you can suggest a different break activity, or ask the child what would feel good right now. Whatever you decide, the activities are not rewards or punishments. They are just a break. This is a strategy a child can learn to use in self-management throughout his or her lifetime.

A Recipe for Making Management Strategies

Now that you have read a few strategies, let us look at what goes into them. You are about to learn the formula for making your own customized strategies. Each factor below is essential to the success of an effective strategy.

The goal is to teach the child a skill that is hard to learn because it is in opposition to her temperament. The new skill will complement her temperament and round out her personality. It will allow her to behave appropriately in a wider variety of situations than she now can, even when a trait is challenged.

The attitude you take is one of acceptance, understanding, and sympathy. Your expectation is that learning takes time. People do not develop skills overnight. Mastery will take many tries, over time. Sometimes a child is not developmentally ready to acquire a skill. When this is the case, expect to put the strategy on hold and try it again later. Remember, we are asking the child to do something that does not come easily, so expect it to take time.

Most people learn better and enjoy learning more when they are involved in multisensory activities, so put some thought into creating strategies which, whenever possible, use touching, moving, seeing, smelling, and tasting as well as listening.

Keep in mind that there is a huge difference between an experience and a lecture. Strategies that rely on too many words and too little involvement tend to be ineffective. Take your child through an active experience that will help her develop the skill. Involve as many senses as you can in the experience.

The experience is more important than the outcome. Why? Because of readiness, or lack of it. The experience should be something reasonably pleasant in which your child willingly takes part. If you end up forcing her, she will soon view the strategy as punishment, which is not your goal.

Incorporate recognition for a job well done. Let your child know that you appreciate her efforts and successes. Take every opportunity to celebrate even little improvements.

The factors above blend together with the five following ingredients to create a well-planned, effective strategy. I have confidence in your creative ability, since some wonderful strategies have come from the mothers and fathers in my program. Here are the five ingredients that go into every management strategy:

- The problem the strategy addresses and a name to call it.
- The temperament trait the strategy is based on.

- The descriptive statement that accompanies the strategy.
- The needed skill the strategy teaches.
- The plan of action that provides an activity for practicing the needed skill.

Note: There may be more than one missing skill, and that is okay. However, if you end up with a whole list, take a look to be sure you are not saying the same thing in different ways. If you are not, and many skills are needed, you may have too big a problem to tackle with one strategy. Can you better address the problem if you break it down into smaller parts? Be specific. For example, "To make eye contact, say hello, and shake hands when introduced" is a clearer statement of skill than to "be polite."

Five Steps for Creating a Management Strategy

1. Choose a problem behavior from among the three you have listed as top priority. Write out the problem as specifically, yet as briefly as you can. Give it a simple name.
2. Identify the temperament trait the behavior is based on. Jot down the underlying traits you think are behind this problem.
3. Using the trait, write out your descriptive statement of the behavior. This is what you will say to convey that you know the task is difficult for the child. Use neutral descriptive language, avoiding words that suggest failure.
4. Write out the needed skill by completing the sentence: "If only he or she could . . . then this problem would be gone." Say exactly what the child will practice doing.
5. Create the "what to do" plan. This is the experience you are setting up.

   Think about when you would like to manage the problem. Do you want to manage this behavior before it happens, as it is happening, or after the fact? How do you want to teach the skill? Based on your knowledge of your child, what would she enjoy doing? Can the child repeat this until she masters the skill? How will you recognize her for her efforts? Keep the experience simple.

When you have completed the planning steps, test the strategy. Try it out. Make adjustments based on trial and error. If it seemed like a good idea, but did not work, save it and try it again later when she may be more ready. If the strategy is one she can use later as she learns to manage herself, so much the better.

Tips to Remember

1. Management strategies are positive discipline techniques designed to teach skills the child needs to behave more appropriately.
2. Management strategies are specific to particular temperament traits.
3. You can design as many management strategies as you need for your unique child.

Fifteen

Putting It All Together

You now have all the information you need to try some new ideas with your child or children. In fact, you may feel like you have too much information and are ready to toss the book and forget about it. If you incorporate only a little of what you have read, it will affect your style of parenting and change the relationship you have with your child for the better. If you are on overload, it is no wonder. Here are eighteen things you have learned. You have:

- gained an understanding of temperament,
- learned to let go of guilt and blame,
- understood the vicious cycle, its effects on the family, and how to interrupt it,
- assessed your child's temperament,
- considered the power of recognition in shaping behavior,

- thought about and taken steps to strengthen your relationship with your child,
- made a comparison of discipline and punishment, and perhaps modified your stand to embrace discipline as being more effective,
- practiced focusing your energy on serious problem behaviors, while letting minor ones go,
- learned to use the "Wait and see" method,
- assessed your own temperament,
- thought about the goodness of fit between your child and his or her environment,
- changed some things in the environment to lessen needless upset and conflict,
- learned that every temperament trait has desirable as well as undesirable potential,
- restated negative and positive labels into supportive statements,
- examined your child's behavior to look for clusters of related problems to make sense of patterns and reduce surprises,
- chosen three problem behaviors on which to begin work,
- mentally rehearsed using the Action Chart, and become confident in your ability to select the most appropriate action for the problem, and
- learned how to construct management strategies for your unique child.

These eighteen choice pieces of learning have the potential to take you and your family more smoothly all the way through your children's teenage years and beyond.

Take the leap to active learning by putting them into practice. I hope you have a better understanding of yourself and of the important people in your life through this introduction to temperament. Have fun and enjoy your new-found family harmony!

Appendix A
Temperament Profile
(Copy and fill in for all family members.)

Activity

High   Low

Adaptability

Slow   Fast

Approach

Quick   Slow

Distractibility

Unaware   Easily diverted

Emotional Sensitivity, to self

Unaware of feelings   Feels strongly

Emotional Sensitivity, to others

Insensitive   Highly tuned in

Intensity

Dramatic   Placid

Mood

Negative, pessimistic   Positive, optimistic

Persistence

Stops easily; gives up   Sticks with a task

Regularity

Predictable   Irregular

Sensory Awareness (Rate all five senses)

Highly aware   Does not notice

Appendix B
Action Chart

(Copy this chart and post it around the house
to help you remember the actions.)

- **Rescue!**
1. Is the child's behavior life-threatening?
2. Protect your child NOW.
3. Later, teach what to do differently.

- **Impose consequences.**
1. Did the child break a rule?
2. State the rule and the consequence for breaking it.
3. Follow through with the consequence.

- **Wait and see.**
1. Is this a minor problem?
2. Stop, think, observe.
3. Ignore the behavior as long as it remains minor.

- **Do as little as possible.**
1. Are you ill, tired, stressed out, or rushed?
2. Do as little as is necessary to bring the situation under control.
3. Wait for a more convenient time to teach new skills.

- **Teach skills.**
1. Do you wish to deal with temperament-based behavior effectively for the long term?
2. Think about what you want the child to learn.
3. Create or select a management strategy to help your child learn how to change a temperament-based behavior.

Index

Skill-building books for parents and children

Without Spanking or Spoiling: A Practical Approach to Toddler and Preschool Guidance by Elizabeth Crary takes the best ideas from four major child guidance approaches and combines them into one practical resource guide. Useful with ages birth to 6 years. 112 pages, $14.95 paper, $19.95 library binding

Temperament Tools: Working with Your Child's Inborn Traits by Helen Neville and Diane Johnson is a godsend for parents of young children. The authors help parents deal with the behavior problems that are common to children of certain temperament types. Useful with birth to 5 years. 128 pages, $13.95 paper, $19.95 library binding

Pick Up Your Socks . . . and Other Skills Growing Children Need! by Elizabeth Crary shows parents how to teach responsibility. A job chart listing average ages kids do household chores helps reduce unrealistic expectations. Useful with ages 3 to 12 years. 112 pages, $14.95 paper, $19.95 library binding

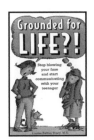

Grounded for Life?! Stop Blowing Your Fuse and Start Communicating with Your Teenager by Louise Felton Tracy, M.A. shows parents how to communicate effectively and avoid problems with their children. *Parents' Choice* award winner. Useful with ages 10 to 18 years. 164 pages, $12.95 paper, $19.95 library binding

Redirecting Children's Behavior by Kathryn Kvols examines reasons children misbehave and offers parents tried-and-true ways to foster closeness, cooperation, and respect in their families. Useful with ages birth to 18 years. 176 pages, $14.95 paper, $19.95 library binding

Help! The Kids Are at It Again by Elizabeth Crary shows parents how to make peace in their families. Children need to learn social skills and parents can teach them with the help of this practical, wise book. Useful with all ages. 96 pages, $11.95 paper, $18.95 library binding

Dealing with Feelings Series by Elizabeth Crary, illustrated by Jean Whitney acknowledges specific feelings and offers children safe and creative ways to express themselves. *I'm Scared, I'm Mad, I'm Excited, I'm Furious, I'm Proud,* and *I'm Frustrated.* Useful with ages 3 to 9 years. Each book, 32 pages, $6.95 paper, $16.95 library binding. Paperback series: $34.75

Children's Problem Solving Series, 2nd edition by Elizabeth Crary, illustrated by Marina Megale helps children learn problem-solving skills. *I Want It, I Can't Wait, I Want to Play, I'm Lost, My Name Is Not Dummy,* and *Mommy, Don't Go.* Useful with ages 3 to 8 years. Each book, 32 pages, $6.95 paper, $16.95 library binding. Paperback series: $34.75

Parenting Press, Inc.
Dept. 806, P.O. Box 75267,
Seattle, WA 98125
In Canada, call Raincoast Books Distribution Co.,
1-800-663-5714

Prices subject to change without notice